# A Rose Among the Ashes

*Discovering Hope*

*When There Doesn't*

*Seem to Be Any*

# A ROSE AMONG THE ASHES

### Debby Fields Jones

© 2007 by Debby Fields Jones. All rights reserved.
2nd Printing 2014

Trusted Books is an imprint of Deep River Books. The views expressed or implied in this work are those of the author. To learn more about Deep River Books, go online to www.DeepRiverBooks.com.

No part of this publication may be reproduced, stored in a retrieval system or transmitted in any way by any means—electronic, mechanical, photocopy, recording or otherwise—without the prior permission of the copyright holder, except as provided by USA copyright law.

Unless otherwise noted, all scriptures quoted in *A Rose Among the Ashes* are taken from the King James 1611 version of the Holy Bible.

Diligent effort has been made to locate the copyright owner of all quoted material in this book.

ISBN 13: 978-1-63269-082-1
Library of Congress Catalog Card Number: 2005908585

Dedicated to the life of Eddie Jones,
my original "rose among the ashes."

# Table of Contents

Foreword ................................................................. ix
Preface .................................................................. xiii
Special Thanks ....................................................... xv
A Rose Among the Ashes ....................................... xvii

## The Hearth of My Heart

Chapter 1: Where's the Fire? ................................... 21
Chapter 2: The Hearth of My Heart ....................... 24
Chapter 3: To Steal and to Destroy ......................... 33
Chapter 4: Resting: The New Action Verb! ............. 36
Chapter 5: We've Got a Big Problem! ..................... 46

## Ashes

Chapter 6: Ashes, Ashes, All Fall Down! ................. 57

Chapter 7: Job and Me ............................................... 62
Chapter 8: Do Ashes Really Have a Purpose? .......... 67
Chapter 9: He Took Me Right to the Edge! ............. 73
Chapter 10: Where's the Hope? ................................ 80
Chapter 11: For Ye Have Need of Patience… .......... 86
Chapter 12: If Not Now…When? ............................ 91
Chapter 13: Remnant Ashes, Too! ............................ 97

## ROSES

Chapter 14: He Gave Me Roses! ............................. 105
Chapter 15: Do Instructions Come With It? ......... 111
Chapter 16: You Want Me to Trust You
    With What, God? ............................................ 120
Chapter 17: Trading Ashes for Roses ..................... 123

A Special Message from Debby .............................. 129
More and More Roses ............................................ 133
The Best Rose of All! ............................................. 137
Endnotes ............................................................... 141

# Foreword

### IN SICKNESS AND IN HEALTH...

There will always be troubles and trials in this life. They can't be escaped. My response to them makes all the difference in the world. *A Rose Among the Ashes* was born as a result of one of the most heartbreaking periods of my life.

My husband, Eddie, was diagnosed with bladder cancer in February 2003. He underwent surgery, and his body was bombarded with radiation and chemotherapy for "clean up" of any microscopic cells. We walked that rough road and I watched what he went through with the treatments.

Only a few months after the first round of treatments ended, tests showed that the cancer had turned into transitional lymphoma and unbelievably jumped to the opposite side of his body. The second regimen of chemotherapy was worse than the first, and I watched the toll it took on Eddie physically and emotionally.

I remember the night I came back into the kitchen from eating supper with our close friends, the two Farmer families, as if it was yesterday. Eddie had not felt like going out, and he stood there with tears in his eyes saying, "I need to tell you something. I've tried to keep it from you, but I can't hold it inside anymore. I can feel knots in my neck and under my left arm." The bottom dropped out of my stomach—again. We called our wonderful pastor and his wife to come and pray with us as we faced more potentially devastating news.

Within a matter of weeks the cancer exploded and created so many complications that my courageous soldier could fight no longer. Eddie's attitude, sense of humor, and faith touched everyone around him, including me.

Because of the road Eddie and I walked together—"in sickness and in health…until death do us part"—I share with you what it takes to face troubles and trials. I want to give to you what God has revealed to me about myself and my faith. If it helps someone else who must walk a similar road, then there is the bright spot.

Some of these pages contain truths I learned walking with God over the years. Other truths have been revealed to me as I moved from line to line, page to page. I have matured more in my relationship with God during this time. It's nothing I've done, except trust God to do what He has promised.

*A Rose Among the Ashes* is intended to be words of inspiration, not a Bible study or book of instruction. These are truths that God has revealed to me prior to and during the writing of this book. When I first wrote the title poem to Eddie, I intended it to be a love poem to him. It was telling the story of how God brought the two of us together. I never dreamed how it would finally be used to be the basis for this book. God has shown me how to use the principle found in the poem to face each of life's trials. He is amazing!

# Preface

I can remember thinking a few weeks ago how nothing really bad had happened in our marriage. Then it did—Eddie has bladder cancer. I really worried about his symptoms for a while, but he had assured me that it was just his regular diagnosis of prostate problems. He finally gave in and went to the doctor with a bladder infection that wouldn't clear up with his normal increase of water intake. Following two rounds of antibiotics and tests, we were given the heartbreaking news. I am going to use this journal to record what God is doing for us.

There is no doubt that God brought Eddie and me together, and I believe He gave us a liberal "grace" period to enjoy as a reward for what I went through getting to Eddie and for our service to His kingdom.

—Excerpts from Debby's journal, March 2003

# Special Thanks

To my precious mother, Willie Mae Fields, for her loving sketch of the rose that appears throughout this book. What a tremendous Christian example she has lived before me. Mother, you have been one of my greatest teachers!

My friends at *Pleasant Word* and *WinePress Publishing*, who patiently guided me through this publishing process to complete a task that I never imagined I would undertake. I am eternally indebted to George Dillaway, my project manager, and Abigail Davidson, publicist.

# A Rose Among the Ashes

So many times I have looked inward to the hearth of my heart and seen ashes scattered about.
Each time the blossom of eternal love had struggled to grow, flames of disappointment would devour the fragile, tiny petals.
I sift among those ashes…struggling one last time to find the roots of everlasting love.
With one thin thread of hope, I hesitantly went to the hearth of my heart
And dug deeply into the cold heap and found—a rose among the ashes.

—Debby Fields Jones

Note from the author: While it's true that "A Rose Among the Ashes" was in fact a love poem to my dear husband, it is also a love poem from God to each of us. Who would even begin to imagine that roses could survive in ashes? God is whispering to you and me, "There is a way to find hope where and when you least expect it."

# The Hearth of My Heart

## Chapter 1

# WHERE'S THE FIRE?

The warmth of the fire fills every corner of the room. The light of the flames prevents shadows from intruding on the feeling of warmth and safety. You can almost hear a soft, gentle sigh of contentment as the crackling fire reaches out to draw you into its embrace. The cold, howling wind on the outside cannot destroy the fire burning within. Strong, protective walls shelter the flame, and it can only be extinguished by being starved or smothered. On the hearth a pile of logs waits to be sacrificed. The tools hang nearby, ready to lend their helping hands.

The door opens and a man rushes in. Pulling the armchair a bit closer to the hearth, the man stretches out and props his feet upon the bricks. The heat is already radiating through his well-worn boots to his chilled toes.

He congratulates himself on his foresight to bring in extra wood before the winter storm hit. *There's enough wood stacked on the hearth to make it to morning.* He stands to throw another log on the fire.

As the familiar sound of the crackling fire gets louder, he reclaims his armchair, settles in his usual position, and smiles. For now, this comfortable spot is his world and the warmth from the fire wraps him in a cozy blanket of contentment.

It's a picture of a room that many would find comforting. This man certainly does.

On the other side of town a cold, dark fireplace anchors an empty room. Nothing except a compacted pile of ashes bears witness that a fire once burned within its walls. A woman enters the room, sighs heavily, shivers, and walks slowly over to the darkened fireplace.

Looking despondently at the ashes, she asks aloud to no one, "Is it worth the effort trying to remove the ashes and lay a fire? Is there anything left to rekindle or is it too late?"

*Life didn't use to be this way. There was a time when I was happy, almost carefree. Where did that go? God, where did You go? How can I ever make sense of life by myself?*

## Where's the Fire?

She reaches for the poker and searches the ashes for remnants of the fire. She stoops to lay her hand on the hearth where the fire once burned brightly before....

Memories of happier times flood her mind as her tears drop one by one to the hearth. Those were the days when she felt the very presence of God in her life, secure in knowing every step was closely matched with His. She could see flashes of days upon days when joy seemed to permeate every corner of their lives—hers and the one she loves. They planned to grow old together doing all those things they had temporarily set aside. Then, one day, it all changed and the one she loves didn't have a choice whether to go or stay. The God she now can't seem to find called him away.

Lost in her memories, she stands. Her shoulders slump from the weight of her burden as she turns to leave the room.

Are you in the first room at this moment in your life? Or are you in the second room, doubting that you can or will ever return to the first one? There is a way to return. I know, because I did. I have been in that second room. Shortly after Eddie's death I found myself digging in the ashes of my life, looking for a flicker of hope.

# Chapter 2
# The Hearth of My Heart

What a strange phrase: "The hearth of my heart"! The heart is the "home" of an individual where commitment, love, pain, compassion, loneliness, indifference, bitterness, sadness, contentment, excitement, and joy live. The "hearth" is the intangible area surrounding the heart, or soul, of a person. It is where our emotions are stored and will ultimately affect the state of our heart. Those emotions can change quickly from one to another.

The hearth of an architectural fireplace is the area that extends from or is connected to the firebox. Because of its adjoining location, the hearth can be cold or warm. It depends on what's happening within the firebox. The "hearth" of my heart likewise reflects the condition and "temperature" of my heart.

God placed His love (the fire) within my heart (the firebox) when I gave my life to Him at the age of nine. "But *his word* was in mine heart as a burning fire shut up in my bones...." (Jeremiah 20:9). His love will always be there (Romans 8:35–39).

Have you ever touched a hearth when a fire is burning brightly in the fireplace? It's warm to the touch because it absorbs the radiating heat from the flames. In the absence of a fire, the hearth takes on the temperature of the room.

Picture a hearth. Tools for tending and wood for feeding the fire are usually located within easy reach, because they are important to the health of the fire. Ashes can also gather on the hearth.

The "hearth of the heart" is an important place in a person. What's on your heart's "hearth"? Are there tools? Wood? Ashes?

## Wood

You need wood to feed the fire. Our wood-burning heater was the only source of heat in our home. We kept a huge stack of winter wood on hand. Eddie usually cut enough to last for the cold months and early spring nights so we could have heat when we needed it.

One particular Christmas Eve, Eddie's youngest brother was supposed to come to our house to put more wood in the heater while we were gone to Birmingham for my family's Christmas celebration. We returned home around 10:00 P.M. and found that Brian had just gotten there to put wood in the heater. The fire was almost out! It had burned all the existing wood and none had been replaced at the right time. Since the temperature was in the low 30s, it took a very long time for the rooms to get warm again.

The wood was there in the carport waiting to be carried in to the heater. The wood couldn't walk in and stack itself on the hearth.

In a similar way the wood represents my faith. It can lie there on the hearth of my heart; but if I don't exercise my faith and put it into action, then it's useless. Peter had faith that he could walk on water to Jesus and stepped out of the boat (Matthew 14:25-33). He did something with his faith.

## Tools

You also need tools. When Eddie worked to revive the dying fire, he poked and moved the burning wood around so air could get under it to allow it to burn. This also made space for more wood to be added. Once the poker had done its job, flames once again burned brightly until more wood was needed. Tending a fire is a continuous circular process: add wood, use the tools, add wood, use the tools, and so on. Eddie's fireplace tools also included a shovel to clean the debris away. The firebox must be cleaned out periodically so the fire can burn correctly. All of these items are equally important.

There have been many times during my life when I have been disappointed in the condition of my heart (the firebox) and its hearth. Sometimes I've allowed the evil one to gain access by not keeping a vigilant watch upon my heart (1 Peter 5:8). And, if *I'm* disappointed, just think how God feels. I am not proud of these times of weakness; I'm just simply trying to be honest with you. You see, experiencing personal trials has taught me that if I don't permit God's strength to guard my fire (Isaiah 41:10), my strength can't withstand the tricks and attacks of the devil.

Since Eddie used the wood to feed the fire and tools to keep it burning dependably, I have to do the same thing with my heart and its hearth. My faith (wood) is stacked and ready to be used, as well as the tools (Bible study and prayer ["poker"], clearing shovel ["sin"]) in that similar circular process described earlier.

Not just any type of wood creates a good fire or sustains heat while burning. I recall a friend of ours having pine trees cut down in his yard. He cut the trees into logs to fit his fireplace. Eddie had to explain to him that pine is not ideal for that use. Pine will burn fast and gives off very little heat. The best wood to use for heat is a hardwood such as oak.

Wood to be stacked on the hearth of my heart resembles this same idea. By loading the hearth of my heart with quick and easy or shallow actions, the pine-like logs that I add to the fire won't sustain me through tough times. It might provide a flash of comfort but nothing for the long haul. I have mistakenly assumed at times that by simply attending Sunday school and worship services I will possess all of the hardwood I need to regularly add to the fire. Although church attendance does help, I can't let that be the only source for gathering wood for my fire. Church attendance alone would be something akin to quick and easy actions like the pine wood. There are six days of living between each Sunday. Wednesday night Bible study definitely helps, but it just won't keep a long-lasting fire going in my heart. I need to gather wood everyday through my personal quiet time.

When I practice careful, whole-hearted response to the Holy Spirit's drawing, I'm building a pile of the hardwoods. Other hardy types of long-burning logs would be dedicated prayer time and meditation. I don't mean an hour of "name that want" but building minute upon minute of searching the Scriptures to discover God's wonderful promises. I like to find a beautiful verse of praise and meditate on it by praying through the natural phrases of that verse. I can also add a period of fasting to the stack.

Obedience is one of those hardwoods that you want on the hearth of your heart. Hardwood provides long-term heat, and that's a very good thing!

A recent experience comes to mind that might help. One night after Eddie died I was having my prayer time with God. As it sometimes happened, I was going through a rough, emotional evening. My grief felt like it was going to overwhelm me and I was on the verge of losing all control. I felt it building like a volcano about to erupt. I was praying for God to speak to me and give me comfort. Turning through the Old Testament, my eyes fell upon a particular verse in the tenth chapter of Daniel. It seemed that verse 15 literally jumped off the page at me. The verse says, "And when he had spoken such words unto me, I set my face toward the ground, and I became dumb."

A compelling feeling came over me that I should lay face down in the floor. I obeyed while imagining what amazing things the God of all creation was going to show me. I told God that I was positioning myself like Daniel and that I wouldn't speak but only concentrate on Him and His goodness. Minutes ticked by as I meditated on God and how wonderful He has been to me. As the clock chimed nine times, I felt released to rise from the floor.

Realization began to dawn on me that peace and comfort had now flooded throughout my entire body. It wasn't that God wanted to show me a vision like He did for Daniel that day. He answered my prayer by redirecting my thoughts from my pain to Him and all that He is to me. I became speechless and did not tell Him any more about me, me, me. I became dumb and thought about Him, Him, Him. The peace and comfort

God imparted to me that night remained with me for many weeks.

It took an act of faith on my part to be obedient during those hours of intense pain and grief. I didn't understand why He wanted me to lie face down at first, but it became abundantly clear afterwards. God may sometimes ask us to do something and we can't understand the importance or the urgency. Be assured that He has a perfect reason, because He knows the outcome if we simply obey.

The last sure-fire way to replenish the stack of best wood is by using how I respond to each life event to bolster my faith and trust in God. Jesus Christ is the author and finisher of our faith. It began with Him and He'll complete it each time He welcomes one of His own to Heaven. My faith is being perfected each time it is exercised. During the two years of Eddie's cancer treatments, he felt like building a fire in our fireplace only a couple of times. I've since stood and looked at the rack of wood on the back patio. You know what's happening to that wood? It's deteriorating. Those carefully cut logs are beginning to break down and rot. Eventually if I try to pick them up, they'll crumble in my hands. Faith, like wood, is not meant to lay idle for very long or it won't get the job done when it's needed.

We have a group of ladies from our church who make a summer pilgrimage to the Gulf Shores area for rest and renewal. It began with a fun idea in 1996, and we were amazed at the true plans God had for us during these times. To commemorate the ten-year anniversary of the first trip, we pledged to do our best not to let anything hinder us from going. The last evening there was a special time for all of us. When one of the original group had gone to be with the Lord, her daughter made her inaugural trip.

There was a discussion during one of our quiet times about how rock altars had impacted different people's lives. Instead of building an altar with rocks representing what each person was turning over to God, we used shells from the beach. Beautiful sea shells were gathered from the shoreline and laid out on the balcony table. We were encouraged to think about what we needed to give to God. It could represent a particular sin in our life that God had revealed during the trip. It could also be a prayer request or need. Each lady could either share what the shell represented or not.

As the Holy Spirit began to move, ladies proclaimed what their shell symbolized. God had already shown me a sin that I needed to recognize and confess to Him. I was anxious about when I was going to receive a certain promised blessing from God. I was permitting this anxiety to consume my waking hours. It was making me miserable. By focusing on the future, I was missing out on enjoying this present time. There was so much to enjoy right under my nose, but I couldn't see it because of this sin. Though Eddie was a huge part of my life, he wasn't my entire life. I have a son, daughter-in-law, three grandchildren, my mother and family, Eddie's family, and a host of friends. And that's just the beginning!

After each one shared what her shell or shells signified we walked down to the beach. Holding hands in a circle, we prayed one more time for our need, relinquishing our burdens to God. We broke apart and stood in the water's edge. I took the shell of my anxiety over God's promise and cast it into the sea. I didn't cast the promise into the waves, but the sin of worrying about it.

Did God honor that act of faith? Yes! Yes! Yes! It felt like a weight had been lifted from my shoulders, and it had. Sin weighs us down and also rots the wood stacked on the hearth of our hearts. Acting on my faith that God would forgive me of my confessed sin (1 John 1:9) added several logs to the growing wood pile. Now when I feel lonely, I just think about that shell that sailed from my hand into God's sea of forgiveness.

# Chapter 3
# TO STEAL AND TO DESTROY

As I mentally flip back through the album pages of my life, I reminisce and rejoice over the snapshots of victory God won in each of my situations. Unfortunately, there are also captured times I didn't keep the fire burning brightly; I allowed complacency to creep in following those victories. I foolishly supposed that "resting in the Lord" meant doing nothing. I should have been a "Mary," sitting at His feet, "choosing the good part" (see Luke 10:38-42).

I learned the hard way that "resting" doesn't mean an absence of Bible study and prayer. I didn't guard my heart (the firebox). While I wasn't paying attention, the one who steals and destroys crept in to rob me of the wood and tools from the hearth of my heart

(John 10:10). If there's neither wood nor tools available, what happens to a fire? It goes out.

It was a gradual thing and didn't happen overnight. Satan is rarely obvious but is clever and sneaky. His ploy is to keep me from realizing that a change is taking place until he has a stronghold in that area (in this case, prayer and Bible study) of my life.

Are you unfamiliar with a stronghold? When a child of God allows the sinful nature to overpower what he or she knows to be right in God's eyes, a stronghold is in place. If the sin is left unrecognized and unrepented, it becomes more the norm than the exception.

Once it finally dawned on me that a stronghold existed in my spiritual life, I had to backtrack to pull it down. I had to make up the lost ground. Pulling down the stronghold meant acknowledging and repenting of my sin and asking God to forgive me for allowing this sin to exist in my life. I had to ask Him to destroy this stronghold. God's power is the only way Satan's stronghold can be destroyed (2 Corinthians 10:3–5).

I can have all the wood (faith) in the world piled up on the hearth, but if I don't do something with it, then what's the use? If my Bible lies on the shelf, what good is it doing in my life? How can God speak precious truths to me? If my prayer life is only to the extent of thanking God for the food I eat or keeping me safe throughout the night, then how can I keep the fire going in my firebox (heart)? God wants me to tell Him what's troubling my spirit, what I need from Him (not necessarily a "wish list"), and how much I love Him.

I must admit that I was guilty. I was resting (foolishly assuming that might mean lying around like a beached whale waiting for someone to come along and shove me back into the water)! Then other times I was busy, busy with stuff! Important stuff! Stuff that I supposed needed my attention. But, sometimes, you have to let one important activity go in order to get the right task accomplished.

# Chapter 4
# RESTING: THE NEW ACTION VERB!

Resting in the Lord requires a certain degree of action. Is this contradictory? Worldly scholars might say *yes*. God says *no*. Understanding what Mary was doing at the feet of Jesus as found in the tenth chapter of Luke might seem a contradiction. Was Mary doing nothing? No. She was gathering wood for the hearth of her heart.

Martha's activity was not necessarily wrong. Working in the kitchen is important. But she was not doing what she should have been doing at *that particular time.* My word! Jesus was in the house! What if that happened today? Would I be off in the kitchen making sandwiches or washing dishes? I think not. I'd want to be right there in the middle of what was going on, hearing what our Lord had to say.

## Resting: The New Action Verb!

Jesus didn't want to take (physical) food that day but desired to give (spiritual) food. Right now in my life God has specifically told me to *wait* and *rest*.

In the midst of the most heartbreaking and devastating time in my life, I resigned my long-time job of teaching Sunday school. God gave me permission to come aside for a while. Teaching fifth and sixth graders each Sunday morning has been a rich blessing to me for more than ten years. I learned so much from them. It was a joy watching the earliest ones reach young adulthood, then marry and have children of their own. But, God told me it was OK to "come out of the kitchen."

My comfortable world was turned upside down. There were things that God needed to reveal to me and help me understand what had happened in my life. I needed to define the shadowy images of the other plans He has for me. I've been a Martha far too long. For now, just call me Mary. I am now sitting at the feet of Jesus.

I recently sang a song at church that includes the following verse.

> Sitting at the feet of Jesus.
> Where can mortal be more blessed?
> There I lay my sin and sorrows
> and when weary, find sweet rest.
> Sitting at the feet of Jesus.
> There I love to weep and pray.
> While I from His fullness gather,
> grace and comfort every day.[1]

Notice the action verbs in this beautiful song. *Laying* my sin and sorrows. *Finding* that sweet, needed rest. *Weeping* and *praying*. *Gathering* grace and comfort every day. *Do you get it now? Sitting* is actually an action verb; it requires *doing*. It's how I gather wood for the fire and use the tools for tending it.

So, how do I gather the wood to be stacked on the hearth of my heart? I try to picture Mary at the feet of Jesus on that special day. I wonder what Jesus was telling her. I won't know in this life, but I'm sure it was just what she needed to hear and learn. Just think what Martha missed while she was in the kitchen. Then she complained to the Lord about her sister.

There are several ways I can gather wood. And, just as Mary did, I sometimes have to prioritize my activities.

Wood-gathering (faith-building) is begun by believing what God has stated. His divine ability to keep His word/promises is confirmed to us in Romans 4:21: "And being fully persuaded that, what he had promised, he *was* able also to perform." His promise is also fulfilled through Jesus in 2 Corinthians 1:20: "For all the promises of God in him [Jesus] *are* yea, and in him [Jesus] Amen, unto the glory of God by us."

Another aspect of wood-gathering can be stepping out on faith (like the famous story of Peter when he walked on the water to Jesus). The following is an example of remarkable wood-gathering for my hearth.

# Resting: The New Action Verb!

As a vocalist, I sang with a group of childhood friends called The Choralaires. The Choralaires had been paying their dues in becoming known in the church singing group circuit by backing up other veteran groups.

We were so excited. It was our first church homecoming as the featured (and only) quartet. New matching outfits were made. New songs were learned. It was time for The Choralaires to stand on their own eight feet. The momentous Sunday morning dawned and we gathered at Dennis and Carole's (brother/sister) home to prepare to leave for the church. I dreaded walking in. What my friends did not know was that I awakened with laryngitis and could barely whisper!

Standing in their living room, we frantically tried to decide what to do. It was too late to call the church's song director because it would leave the church without a group for the homecoming services. Other quartets we knew would also have bookings since it was the height of homecoming season. The only thing we could do was *pray*. And, pray we did. We asked God to do what He does best: make a way and allow us to serve in the manner He had called.

We traveled to the church and immediately began to set up our sound equipment. I refrained from trying to talk but worried all the same. How would God work it out? As usual, we found a quiet room where we could hold hands in a circle to pray for the service. When it came my time to pray, nothing would come out.

Dennis, Carole, and Shelia allowed me a few moments to voice my prayer in my heart. Nevertheless, we went to the sanctuary to await our time to sing. We said nothing about my voice.

The Choralaires were introduced and we climbed the stairs to the stage to sing. Carole played the introduction to the first song. We smiled at each other, stepped up to the microphones, took a deep breath and opened our mouths to sing praises to the God of all creation. The much-practiced three-part harmony came bursting forth loud and clear!

After the first song ended, Dennis asked me if there was anything I wanted to say as testimony leading to the second song. You know what happened? I couldn't say the first word! Dennis had to explain to the congregation about my laryngitis. The miracle was this. I could sing, but I couldn't speak. The Choralaires stepped out in faith on that fateful Sunday morning and God honored that step. While there might be a medical explanation as to how I could sing but not talk, it was our unshakeable belief that God had made a way. That was the shining star in our hearts!

I believe an armload of wood was gathered that day.

- I stepped out on faith, secure that God would make a way for us to sing (James 1:6).

- Believing that God had called us into this ministry and would take care of us, we were enabled to touch hearts during the service in more ways than through music. The congregation saw how we had felt compelled to trust God and come ahead even though one member couldn't even whisper the first word. God assures us that He will never leave us or forsake us (Hebrews 13:5). He promises that He will always be with us.

Each time I trust God and act on what He instructs me to do, I add another log to the hearth. Every time I am obedient to the urging of the Holy Spirit to take the step of faith, my stack of logs grows higher. Faith (wood) is replenished when it is used.

The tools on the hearth (Bible study and prayer) can also help build the wood pile. The more I know the heart of God, the easier it is to believe His words. It helps me have the faith I need to walk through each day or to search for hope in the midst of my awful circumstance.

God sets great store by one's heart. It is difficult to find one perfect reference verse for that statement. God has much to say about the heart (positive and negative) in the Scriptures. Research the word "heart" in a Bible concordance. One verse I thought summed up a lot of what I'm talking about is found in Psalm 57:7: "My heart is fixed, O God, my heart is fixed: I will sing and give praise." The writer found it necessary to state "my heart is fixed" twice. It must be doubly important for my heart to stay focused on God. Satan will try to divert my concentration so that when trials come my way I will focus on the gravity of the situation and not the ultimate outcome.

Though the quartet days are long past, I sing solos at church. Honestly, it was rather difficult to get back up there the first time after Eddie's death. It was hard to go back to the choir and sit in my old place among so many friends. What did I have to sing about? My heart was shattered. Eddie's illness didn't turn out like we thought it would. I hardly had the strength to walk from the pew to the pulpit; I wanted to just sit and let others do the work of offering up praise. At one point, I even thought, *I don't want to sing anymore. God, you used the gospel music ministries of The Choralaires* [my quartet] *and The Bridgemen Quartet* [Eddie's group] *to bring Eddie and me together. That's how we met! My reason's gone! If you used our music to bring us together, then how can I sing if the one you gave me is no longer physically here?* I had to admit to myself that my reason for singing did not go to the grave. My reason for singing—Jesus Christ—rose from the grave and is now seated at the right hand of God.

But Satan wanted to take away my desire to sing. The deceiver desired to sift me like wheat as Christ spoke to Peter in Luke 22:31–32. Let my thanks and praises abound because Jesus has prayed for me that my faith does not fail. Eddie was not my reason to sing. God instructs us in the latter part of Luke 10:20: "but rather rejoice, because your names are written in heaven." What's interesting is that in the first part of that verse we see other circumstances that mankind would think would be reasons to rejoice ("that the spirits are subject unto you…"). Staying focused on the true reason for rejoicing and praising is critical to building faith.

I have so much to sing about and to praise God for His blessings. It was a Herculean effort, but God helped me to stand once again to sing for Him. I knew I must sing again because my music is a precious gift from God. I don't want to lose it. The gift is to praise the Most High God and allow Him to touch others through it. I long to lift up the name of Jesus through song.

Since I had once sung in a gospel quartet, I was accustomed to giving a word of testimony before certain songs. I usually do when I sing at my church because that's when I feel most led to testify. God gives me words of testimony to also serve as an introduction to the song. I couldn't say anything at first (after Eddie's death) if I wanted to have enough control over my emotions to sing. In my aching, worldly flesh, I only wanted to remind everyone that *my heart is hurting. My wonderful husband is dead. We were supposed to have more than twenty-eight years together!* I knew in my heart that saying those things would be selfish and not glorifying to God. So, I just didn't say anything. I let the song do the talking. But, that's OK. I think my spiritual family understood. The words of testimony eventually came again when there was something God really wanted me to say. I've had to learn to take baby steps.

A verse heavily underlined in my Bible is 1 Peter 1:7: "That the trial of your faith, being much more precious than of gold that perisheth, though it be tried with fire, might be found unto praise and honour and glory at the appearing of Jesus Christ." My heavenly Father assures me that He doesn't view the trial of my faith as an insignificant event. It's not way down on His priority list. The trial of my faith tugs at God's heart strings.

As I think about the months leading up to and even those since Eddie's death, it often seems as if I am looking at someone else's life. I love to read novels based upon historical events. I have also devoured the wonderful faith fiction books of Karen Kingsbury. In fact, it was during the reading of two of her books that God confirmed the writing and publishing of the one you now hold.

During my time of grief, it is like I'm rereading the words from the pages of my favorite novel. And if I truly bare my soul to you, my friend, it sometimes feels like Eddie never existed. Or perhaps was a character in a book I had read. He was such a dynamic part of my life and now he's not here. I told one of my friends that when Eddie and I had been married a long time, my life with my parents seemed to fade away. And now, I've set out on another leg of my journey. That chapter of my life is completed and it's time to turn the page to begin another.

## Chapter 5
# WE'VE GOT A BIG PROBLEM!

Everything in my life that was normal shattered into tiny fragments piercing my heart. Here I thought the report would reveal something that could easily be treated or at worst, corrected through surgery. Never in my wildest dreams did I for one second anticipate the possibility of cancer! I can remember just looking the doctor in his face, waiting for him to say, "But, I don't think we have anything to worry about." Those words never came. Instead, his phrase, "We've got a big problem," kept reverberating in my head and bouncing off the hospital room walls. It even took several minutes for my brain to process what he was saying before tears spilled down my cheeks.

Just a handful of words from Eddie's doctor felt like an atomic bomb exploding in my heart and mind. The only other person in the hospital room with me that morning hearing those words was my loving heavenly Father.

The walls began to close in on me. If Eddie and I had had any idea that the scope would reveal bad news, I would have asked someone, anyone, to come with us. For a few minutes, I had never felt so alone. I didn't know what to do first. After the doctor left the room, I immediately called our son to break the news to him. It would take Jeremy almost two hours to arrive at the hospital since he and Susan were then living in Auburn, Alabama.

*Help me, God. I can't believe this is happening to us!* I next called our close friends, Jerry and Rhonda Sanford. I told them not to let anyone else know just yet since I felt like Eddie would want to tell his mother in person. But I knew that they would immediately begin interceding on our behalf. While I can only recall crying out to the Lord to help us, I know now that He was already orchestrating and ordering our steps through this valley. The Holy Spirit carried my heart's groanings directly to the throne of God who knew just what we would need in the coming days. By the time Eddie was brought back to the room and coming out from under the anesthesia, God had begun pouring His peace and comfort over me.

My heart is the firebox and the fuel I put into it is important. It responds to what I do. Not long after Eddie's cancer diagnosis, I felt dead inside. Our peaceful and stable world had been turned upside down in a matter of moments. I felt bound and paralyzed. I had allowed the fire in my heart's firebox to burn down so low that it couldn't warm the hearth.

Slowly and painfully it began to dawn on me that I had to do something about the way I felt. I had to pray for myself before I could effectively pray for my husband. I began to cry out to God to break the chains that were binding me so I could praise Him. God is always listening for His child's cry, and during that prayer time He began to do a mighty work in my heart. In a few minutes I began to feel a load being lifted from my soul. God directed me to Jeremiah 40:4: "And now, behold, I loose thee this day from the chains which *were* upon thine hand...."

Hindsight is always better. I can look back now and see clearly how I had permitted God's fire to burn down too low to provide heat to warm my life. The embers from a once roaring blaze were barely glowing. I had neglected my Bible study and prayer time. Those are the two most important tools for tending my heart's fire.

Often watching Eddie work with the fire in our fireplace, I saw he used a shovel for removing the remnants of past fires and a poker for stirring up the embers. I had not asked God to "shovel" out the sin in my life. Neither had I used a "poker" of prayer to rouse my praise and commitment to Him.

# We've Got a Big Problem!

The Lord spoke loudly to my heart on the last Sunday in November of 2005 through words in our church bulletin. He showed me I was not using my fireplace tools in equal proportions with the wood.

> Little of the Word with little prayer is death to the spiritual life.
> Much of the Word with little prayer gives a sickly life.
> Much prayer with little of the Word gives emotional life.
> But, a full measure of both the Word and prayer each day gives a healthy and powerful life![2]

Since I had plenty of alone time at night, I decided to put it to use. I made a conscious effort to set aside 8:00 to 9:00 each night for prayer time. That seemed to work best for me. I look back and see what was going on in those early days of my prayer time. I was not balancing prayer with Bible study and I was winding up with an *emotional* prayer time. Yes, prayer is important; but so is the Word of God. I think I was praying and then looking for scripture to back up my petitions.

I discovered it was more productive to turn to God's Word *first*, let Him direct me to a particular verse or verses and then pray. Sometimes I reverse, beginning my prayer to cleanse my own heart ("If I regard iniquity [sin] in my heart, the LORD will not hear *me*" [Psalm 66:18]). Then I prayed as I felt led by the Holy Spirit.

Perhaps I might meditate on a certain verse He has given me. I have to keep in mind that prayer is not to change God's will but mine. Prayer is to make sure that I am in line with what He wants. I can truthfully say that my specific hour with God is more fruitful and special since I am trying to balance the "full measure of both the Word and prayer each day." It makes God's job a whole lot easier when my heart and mind are making a conscious effort to be in tune with His.

Some wonderful side effects from my now balanced prayer time include: a return to once again praying more for others than for myself, certain truths and thoughts for this book, help to begin my understanding of what happened with Eddie's death, an ease in the sorrow I have felt, the ability to wait on God, insight into His future plans for me, and beautiful grace and comfort for every day.

In praying for others, I have made a conscious effort to commit a portion of Monday night's prayer to embrace my church family. Since we are creatures of habit and Northside Baptist Church is not a large congregation, I can visualize where each family sits during worship service. I then pray for that family by name as my mind walks between each pew. My petitions often include a specific request they may have shared or to simply pray for God to meet their needs and bless them. It gives me a special feeling when I have called their names in prayer. They prayed for us so much during our dark valley that I count it a privilege to be able to return the love.

Another side effect of the balanced prayer time seems to be that my understanding of Eddie's death has become more of a peaceful acknowledgement in my heart that God's will was fully accomplished. It's an acceptance of the course of events during those two years. I may never fully know until I am face to face with my King and I can live with that. I am no longer tormented by this. I can now go many days without breaking down when I think of Eddie or gaze at a picture of Eddie, Jeremy, and me capturing our family on Jeremy and Susan's wedding day.

Ideas run through my mind about my future. As I write, it is often similar to someone dictating as I type. Other thoughts come during my quiet time with the Lord. The opportunity of a music ministry seems to be blossoming. All of the answers are not complete, but I am confident that God will reveal all to me in His time.

## The Never-fail Recipe

The recipe for that perfect cake Grandma serves during the holidays or Mom's famous covered dish casserole for church functions have specific measurements of ingredients. If not followed correctly, the end result will not be something pleasing to eat. The cake may not rise properly. The icing may be too thin or too thick to spread. The casserole may taste bland if not seasoned in the right amounts.

It shames me to think about how I had allowed the fire of God within me to burn so low. I had not been practicing what I taught to my class all of those years. I didn't have the right measure of prayer and Bible study to have that "healthy and powerful life." *Thank you, God. You never left me and you didn't give up on me. You just urged me to return to the Potter's house so that my vessel could be mended and made useful once again.*

So, here's my recommendation based upon what I have experienced and what God has revealed in His Word to all of us. You, too, can have what it is buried deep within my soul.

Recipe for a Healthy Spiritual Life

1 Clean Heart
1 Heaping Cup of Sincere Prayer Time
1 Heaping Cup of Bible Study Time
2 Listening Ears
2 Eyes Fixed on the Lord
2 Hands Lifted in Praise
1 Voice Declaring God's Majesty

Directions: After the heart has been thoroughly cleansed, combine remaining ingredients in equal amounts on a daily basis. Plus nothing, minus nothing…

God will do the rest.

## THE HEARTH OF MY HEART CHECKLIST

Let's look at your "firebox" and "hearth." We want to fully understand the importance of each component that makes up your hearth and heart. I invite you to think carefully about each one of the questions. Be honest with yourself. This is your time to take an inventory of your heart.

1. Am I familiar with a place deep within my being that holds the emotions of my life?
   - Are there times in my life I feel joy, contentment, and peace (warmth)?
   - Do I recognize that I experience suffering, pain, and despair (coldness)?
   - Do I have a spiritual fire burning within me?
   - Has the fire burned down very low?
2. Have I prepared myself with the spiritual tools essential for tending the fire in my heart?
   - Do I use these tools in an equal amount on a daily basis?
   - Do I only use these tools and add wood when the fire is about to go out?
   - Is this roaring blaze almost gone out, and do I need to do something about it?

# Ashes

# Chapter 6

# ASHES, ASHES, ALL FALL DOWN!

How many times have we heard children sing the song, "Ring around the Rosy"? How many times on the playground did I drop to my knees in the dirt as the circle of my friends chanted that line? Now that I think about it, I really didn't understand what we were singing or its meaning. Oh well, it was just a game to play. What does a kindergartner know about ashes?

Ashes are the leftovers after something has burned. What exactly are the "ashes" in our lives? Ashes are those times when you feel like the foundation of your world has crumbled into broken pieces or simply "gone up in smoke." The type of ashes may be a storm in everyday living that's trying to blow you off God's course. You are the only one who knows what the ashes are in your life. I can only tell you what *my* ashes are right now and have been in the past.

Ashes hurt! They can be personal or family tragedies. Critical or terminal illness usually can be perceived as ashes. A child of God walking out of the center of God's will can be a "mound" of ashes with far-reaching consequences (just meet the prodigal son in Luke 15). Ashes are normal. It's OK. Ashes help make us who we are. To borrow a time-worn cliché: they can either "make us" or "break us." When wind gets into dry ashes, they are scattered abroad. They seem to become almost non-existent. One speck of ash can hardly be seen even though it is still there. If you're not careful, ashes can turn into cold, dense heaps upon the hearth of your heart. They become saturated from tears. Not cleansing tears falling to wash them away but tears of bitterness flowing from a cold heart allowing the ashes to pack down and settle into a hardened crust.

Remember all the times you've had something in your eye but couldn't see what it was? What pain it caused! Ashes must be dealt with, and that's hard to do. It's usually easier or necessary for the moment to ignore them. Have you allowed the Father's breath to blow and scatter the ashes of pain in your life or let those cleansing tears wash them away? Have you taken that first step toward the hearth of your heart? If you will take the first one, the Lord will make the rest of them with you.

## Ashes, Ashes, All Fall Down!

God gives us ashes. You may have even screamed this question to the four corners of the earth: *Why did God let this happen to me?* How can a loving heavenly Father let ashes sift into the life of one of His children?

There's more than enough Scripture that attempts to explain this complex question. In 1 Peter 4:12–13, God wrote: "Beloved (it thrills me to my toes when God calls us "beloved"), think it not strange concerning the fiery trial which is to try you, as though some strange thing happened unto you: But rejoice, inasmuch as ye are partakers of Christ's sufferings; that, when his glory shall be revealed, ye may be glad also with exceeding joy."

Now let's see if we can get this straight in our minds. We shouldn't think it is strange when problems come our way. That's everyday life. Sometimes, it's *big* problems. All right, we can handle a few of those scattered along the journey. But rejoice? Is God telling you that you should be happy that you have problems?

You don't have to shout the roof off because your world stopped spinning, but the child of God can lift his or her hands in praise that there is Someone to turn to for help. Without the trial how can God reveal His glory and give you exceeding joy? Christ suffered for us on the cross of Calvary and in many instances along the way. Should I be any better than He? Christ's gift resulted in salvation for mankind. My suffering can turn into something special, too.

God continues to bring the story of Job to my mind. Let's take a quick review of Job's story. In chapter one, God tells us that Job "was perfect and upright, and one that feared God, and eschewed evil." Job wasn't terrified of the Lord, but he had a reverent respect and awe for His deity. Job did his best to live a life that pleased God.

Job may sound like someone you know, someone in your church or workplace, the neighbor next door, a relative, a close friend. God had blessed Job with family and earthly wealth (Job 1:2–3). However, I believe we sometimes tend to forget about the spiritual warfare that rages above our heads (Job 1:6–12).

The battle between good and evil has been going on since the most beautiful angel Lucifer desired to be God's equal and was cast from Heaven (Isaiah 14:12–15). This war destroyed the perfect peace and fellowship in the Garden of Eden. Jesus even told His disciple and us in Luke 22:31–32 that "Satan hath desired *to have* you, that he may sift *you* as wheat." But, the precious promise that follows in verse 32 assures us that Jesus has prayed for each of us that our faith would be a sustaining power when those bad things happen to good people. Jesus also added that we should in turn strengthen others.

Because Job's faith did not falter, his testimony has strengthened countless hearts down through the ages and will continue to do so as long as his book of the Bible is read.

## ASHES, ASHES, ALL FALL DOWN!

In the span of a day, one messenger after another came to Job to relay the bad news of the loss of his material possessions and his family (Job 1:13–19). What did our friend do? The Scriptures tell us Job humbled himself, fell down, worshipped God, *and* blessed the name of the Lord. Verse 22 tells us that in all that happened to Job in that one day, he did not rail against God for his tragedies. Job did not even know about the 1 Peter 4:12–13 verses either!

God even allows Satan to test Job again, save taking his life, in chapter two. Job's wife doesn't help the situation (verse 9). Here's a brother in Christ down and out. Let's see how much more we can pound him deep into the ground! We tend to jump to a conclusion and ask, "Wonder what God's punishing him for?" Now, look closely at the latter part of verse 8 in chapter 2. Where does Job sit down? Among the ashes! The Bible tells us that Job still did not "sin with his lips" (verse 10).

Let us now fast-forward to chapter 42 of the Book of Job. God begins to move and speak about His servant, Job. Verse 10 tells us, "And the LORD turned the captivity of Job, when he prayed for his friends: also the LORD gave Job twice as much as he had before...So the LORD blessed the latter end of Job more than his beginning (verse 12)...So Job died, *being* old and full of days" (verse 17). That's quite a spectacular ending to a story that began with such unimaginable heartache.

# Chapter 7
# JOB AND ME

I frequently stop to reflect on how God's hand has moved in my life over the years.

Before I married Eddie, I was engaged to another young man. Just a couple of months before our wedding date, he was involved in a horrific crime that ended the life of a young girl. He confessed to me and I had to testify against him during his trial. I asked my pastor why he thought God had chosen me, out of all the other young women around me, to bear that burden. After all, I wasn't the first lady this young man had dated or even been engaged to.

That wise and precious man of God looked at me with compassion in his eyes and said, "Debby, God knew your shoulders were the only ones that could carry this burden." What a tremendous compliment for a child of

God! After thirty years, I am still humbled by his answer and God's confidence in me.

Remember Job's saga? God asked Satan that critical day, "Hast thou considered my servant Job…?" The Lord and our adversary had quite a conversation that day about Job.

God even goes further with His description of Job's character when He says, "that *there is* none like him in the earth, a perfect and an upright man…." (verse 8).

Then Satan challenges God's perception of Job: "Doth Job fear God for nought?" (verse 9). "Hast not thou made an hedge about him, and about his house, and about all that he hath on every side? Thou hast blessed the work of his hands, and his substance is increased in the land" (verse 10). "But put forth thine hand now, and touch all that he hath, and he will curse thee to thy face" (verse 11).

Use your imagination to visualize Satan standing before the Lord as this conversation takes place. Satan has been on the prowl looking to get into some kind of mischief. The Lord wants us to be on our guard because Satan is always on the job "seeking whom he may devour" (1 Peter 5:8). That means he wants to utterly destroy us. Why, he's at his happiest when I am sad, weary at heart, or disappointed at God.

But when bad stuff happens to Christians, "the God of all grace, who hath called us unto his eternal glory by Christ Jesus, after that ye have suffered a while, make you perfect, stablish, strengthen, settle *you*" (1 Peter 5:10). I am not made perfect as in without flaw, but I have matured more in my walk with the Lord. I am firmly established, or set solidly, in His will. My weariness of heart is replaced by His strength, and my mind is more settled and experiencing God's peace.

I am confident, from God's forthright comments about His servant, that Job did possess everything he needed on that sorrowful day in his life. All that Job needed was God, and by having God, Job was perfect: established, strengthened, and settled.

God knew the outcome of Job's trial. God plainly describes Job's heart and life in the very first verse. And, Satan is well aware of the power and protection of God (Job 1:10). Had God not allowed this test of Job, the Bible might have ended with Esther 10:3. Then, where would we be?

God knew what the outcome of my life would be as well. A few weeks after my marital plans billowed in smoke God spoke to the heart of three of my long-time friends and me, calling us into a gospel music ministry. For me, this was a rose among the ashes of my broken relationship. Things seemed to fall perfectly into place and our group, The Choralaires, began traveling from church to church to carry the message of God's salvation to the hopeless. We knew the Lord had brought us together to share His love with His children. We became members of the Alabama Gospel Quartet Association, and in August of 1976, I met the man of my dreams and prayers. Eddie Jones of The Bridgemen Quartet was the second rose among my recent ashes.

In Job 42:10, after all Job had been through, he prayed for his friends. God made him prosperous again and gave him twice what he had before.

While the anticipation of marriage to one young man turned into a pile of ashes, *two* roses were waiting in those ashes to be discovered—a gospel music ministry and my precious Eddie. I didn't recognize this concept of ashes and roses until the ashes of Eddie's illness and death settled on the hearth of my heart.

Isn't it humbling to know that God and Satan could be having a "Job-like" conversation about you or me? Could God respond to Satan with, "Hast thou considered my servant Debby (or insert your name here)?"

Don't forget God's comment about not thinking it strange about the fiery trial happening to you. It probably happens more that we realize or want to know. You've heard the old adage, Ignorance is bliss. Sometimes I really like to be blissful! I prefer not to know!

Verses from Job's story are frequently used during funeral services. But, Job's story is for the living. It's a story of Job's life not his death. Out of the forty-two chapters in the Book of Job, God only devoted three straightforward words to Job's death. "So Job died...." (Job 42:17). Then God encourages us that Job was, "old and full of days." See, I told you, Job's story was for the living!

Job 42:10 explains that after Job prayed for his friends, the Lord made him prosperous again and gave him twice as much as he had before.

Through this verse God has graciously given me a glimpse of one of His plans for me and confirmed some of it so that I might be comforted during this time of healing. I stand on His promise and frequently remind Him during my prayer time of what He has declared to me. God doesn't forget, but I might.

Many people have asked, "How can a loving heavenly Father let ashes sift into the life of one of His children?"

The honest answer is, *I don't completely know*. I'm not God. It's really not God's will for me to always fully understand or see the big picture. But, I do know this. Glancing back over my shoulder at the photo album of my life, I have seen some of the most precious roses come out of the ugliest heaps of ashes. You are now holding one of my recent roses in your hands, and it's my pleasure to share it with you.

# Chapter 8

# Do Ashes Really Have a Purpose?

Maybe that's the answer to the question: "How can a loving heavenly Father let ashes sift into the life of one of His children?" God's Word gives us verse after verse of promise about His plan. Sometimes God's plan appears as different words in the Bible: *thoughts, purpose, will.* Yet, they are ultimately pointing toward His use of my life. In our office at Jacksonville State University, we have goals and objectives that assist the University in carrying out its mission to the community. We have goals and subsequent objectives in place for achieving the end result. At the end of the year, we present a report proving that our goals were met. We must also state how our success is measured.

God does the same thing. His goal is to fashion me into a mature Christian. He then has events/objectives set in place to bring about His goal.

In the twenty-ninth chapter of Jeremiah, words from this "weeping prophet" are sent to Hebrew children who had been carried away captive to Babylon. God reassured them and us today that "I know the thoughts that I think toward you, saith the LORD, thoughts of peace, and not of evil, to give you an expected end. Then shall ye call upon me, and ye shall go and pray unto me, and I will harken unto you. And ye shall seek me, and find *me*, when you shall search for me with all your heart. And I will be found of you, saith the LORD: and I will turn away your captivity, and I will gather you from all the nations, and from all the places whither I have driven you, saith the LORD; and I will bring you again into the place whence I caused you to be carried away captive" (Jeremiah 29:11–14). A parent punishes a naughty child so that hopefully the child will think twice before committing the same transgression again. God, our heavenly Father, does the same to His children. Sometimes ashes exist as a result of my living contrary to what's right in God's eyes. If nothing else, my close relationship with God is broken, my spiritual growth is stunted, and I cannot hear His voice in my heart.

"For the scripture saith unto Pharaoh, Even for this same purpose have I raised thee up, that I might shew my power in thee, and that my name might be declared throughout all the earth" (Romans 9:17).

As much as a loving parent's instinct automatically wants to protect a child from having to experience the problems of life, we have to let him or her learn from mistakes and troubles. If God shields me from life's ups and downs, then I can never fully comprehend what He is capable of bringing me through. When the seas were hammering the boat carrying the disciples and Jesus in Matthew 8:23–27, these mortal men looked at the dire situation they were in and not who was on board with them. Upon being admonished for their lack of faith and witnessing the stilling of the raging sea, "the men marveled, saying, What manner of man is this, that even the winds and the sea obey him!" The power of Jesus was demonstrated in the midst of a horrendous storm! God is ready, willing, and able to demonstrate His power in my situation and all He asks in return is that His name be glorified. Give credit where credit is due!

Accepting that God knows what is best for me is sometimes hard to do. "And he that searcheth the hearts knoweth what *is* the mind of the Spirit, because he maketh intercession for the saints according to *the will of God*" (Romans 8:27). Verse 28 goes further to encourage you and me that everything (good and/or bad) is going to work together for ultimate good.

It is easy for a friend to say, "God knows what He is doing and He won't put more on you than you can bear." You know the drill. You've heard it from the pulpit, the Sunday school teacher, the deacons, well-meaning friends, etc.

You may say to yourself, "They're not the one with my problem! What do they know about what I am going through? How do they know how I feel?" They don't. Individuals react differently to each situation or problem, and we are all at different relationship levels with God.

There's only One who knows just how you are hurting, and He's the only One who can give complete peace and hope beyond all understanding. As a cherished friend, Blaine Galliher, told me soon after the home-going of my beloved husband of twenty-eight-plus years, "Deb, only He [God] can reach down deep enough where you are hurting to ease the pain."

Blaine and I were talking on the phone one evening after he had received my email about Eddie's death. We had worked together for a couple of years at Jacksonville State and our similar faith in the Lord had quickly forged a bond of friendship between us. Out of all the words of encouragement he spoke during that telephone conversation, it was his simple statement of God reaching down deep enough to ease the pain that stuck with me.

How true Blaine's words were, and I've often quoted them again to myself over the months following Eddie's death. Like a lot of women, I have always counted on a set of loving arms to hold me when I hurt. I was physically alone at my kitchen table the night Blaine and I spoke, but it was like I was being held and hugged while we talked. That's the beauty of the miracle of God that moved over me that night. No arms were actually holding me. The Holy Spirit wrapped me in the love of God and my friend.

As children, we run to our moms, dads, or grandparents when we have a boo-boo. Later on, if we are fortunate to have a close pal like I did in my best friend, Shelia Owens Sanford, then hugs are usually available to help ease the pain (especially during those rough teenage years when there is so much "girl stuff"). I was then blessed to have had a husband who was always there for me and who was quick to embrace me when I was down. Yes, I've continually had comforting earthly arms to hold me whenever needed...until now.

I have caring friends I can reach for, a great pastor who is only a phone call away, and a loving son and daughter-in-law. I know the pure joy of a grandson reaching out those little arms for his nana to take and hold him. But I don't have the special one God gave me to be the other half of me. Eddie was the one who could tell just from the tone of my voice that my heart was breaking or that I was upset. One look at my face would alert him of my distress.

Fortunately, there is One other in my life who knows me even better than Eddie did: my heavenly Father. He knows my thoughts. He knows my heart. He doesn't even have to look at my face to know that something is wrong. He doesn't have to hear it in my voice. Blaine's words echo in my mind again: "Only He [God] can reach down deep enough where you are hurting to ease the pain."

There are times of loneliness, weariness, or longing that I feel the warmth of God's arms gathering me up closer to Him. I can feel His cheek next to mine. I can almost hear Him shushing me like a mother to her child and telling me that everything will be all right. It's not that I don't feel the love of God all through my life, I do everyday. But, God is gracious and gives me a double portion of His warmth when I cry out to Him.

# Chapter 9

# HE TOOK ME RIGHT TO THE EDGE!

God has taken me right to the edge!

When we heard the tragic news that Eddie's cancer was back for the *third* time in two years, he and I made plans to travel to M. D. Anderson Cancer Center in Houston, Texas. This trip took place just a few weeks before Eddie went home to be with the Lord. In fact, he entered our local hospital for the first of two times on Friday after we returned home on Tuesday.

A telephone conversation between Jeremy, our son, and me periodically replays in my mind. During that conversation and many others during the two years, Jeremy and I tried to encourage each other. I knew that it was my job to give him the words to help him deal with his father's illness. After all, I was the mother. But my son had great wisdom and often was the one who encouraged me and gave me strength.

I usually shared with him the latest scriptures of promise that God had shown me. In turn, Jeremy always voiced his faith that everything would work out OK. "It's just another bump in the road." Jeremy liked to quote one of his dad's famous lines of encouragement. How many times had Eddie said those same words to us? Just Jeremy's assurance that his faith was strong helped me to keep going. It would thrill my heart to hear him say, "Yes, Momma, I believe that we're going to be all right."

Up until a morning in early April of 2005, Jeremy encouraged me with many of the usual faith statements that we had heard for years in church. But nothing can ever erase Jeremy's wisdom to me that particular morning. I witnessed, first hand, how God gave him something new and a deeper insight into faith. This was not something either one of us had ever heard before. I was awed by the level of his Christian maturity by what God revealed to him.

Jeremy told me that God continued to bring to his mind the story of Abraham's sacrifice as told in the twenty-second chapter of Genesis. Abraham had finally received his promised son and then was put to an unbelievable test of his love for God.

In response to the voice of God, Abraham took the most precious gift he had, his son, and journeyed to the land of Moriah. There, he prepared to give Isaac back to God, the One who had bestowed this most cherished gift. As Abraham and Isaac travel to the appointed place, the son asks his father about the absence of the lamb. Isaac was well-aware that a living lamb was to be slain as a sacrifice to God (verse 7). Abraham reassures his precious Isaac that "God would provide himself a lamb...."(verse 8). I cannot even begin to imagine the pain in Abraham's heart as he attempted to appear as normal and encouraging as possible even though this man knew his son was supposed to be the sacrifice.

Abraham follows God's instructions. He lays the wood in order upon the altar that he has just built. He binds Isaac, his promised son, and lays him on top of the wood. The loving father then takes a knife and raises it to give Isaac back to God in the ultimate act of obedience to his Lord.

As though it were a scripted Hollywood movie, the angel of the Lord calls unto him from out of heaven. Calling Abraham by name to halt the sacrifice, he tells him not to hurt Isaac, "for now I know that thou fearest God, seeing thou hast not withheld thy son, thine only *son* from me" (verse 12).

Jeremy: "Momma, God took Abraham right to the edge."

Me: "I know, Jeremy."

Jeremy: "I believe God is taking us right to the edge with Daddy's cancer. God is testing our love and trust in Him."

God did just that. He took His trusted servant right up to the edge of the cliff but would not let him fall over the side.

What do you think was running through Abraham's mind and heart that day? He might have been asking some of the same questions you or I would be screaming: "Does God know what He's asking of me? Why is He asking me to do this? What part of His redemptive plan could this possibly play?"

Abraham might have even thought, *God, this is the son You promised me. How can I be the father of many nations if I sacrifice my only son?* Of course, this story is only one of the many Old Testament pictures of the plan for the sacrifice God himself would later make, offering His only son.

Only a few days before we flew to Houston, I had been invited to share my music and testimony with a group of ladies at nearby Union Grove Methodist Church. Knowing our travel plans, they unselfishly gave me the option of canceling at the last minute or coming on to meet with them. I felt the Holy Spirit urge me to keep the commitment. I talked to them about God taking us "right to the edge." I didn't realize then that I wasn't really close to the edge yet. I'm glad now that I was still in the dark.

I have been to the edge. God took me there and kept me safely under His protection. I've learned that He alone knows where the edge is and how close I will have to come.

You know what is so ironic about this metaphor?

Debby Jones is deathly afraid of being at the edge of anything without substantial support to keep her from falling. I can't even lean too far to look over the side of the eleventh floor of the library on our campus at Jacksonville State University. I refuse to stand next to the glass to look down when traveling in one of those glass elevators. Eddie tried to help me climb the old fire tower on Dugger Mountain when we were first married so that I could see all of Piedmont. I couldn't make it past the second flight because of the sparse iron railings and wide-open steps. During each of the two failed attempts, I began to hyperventilate and Eddie had to help me down. I gave up on seeing Piedmont from the fire tower. I'll just have to be content to look at it from the street level.

As much as I would like to see the Grand Canyon, I know better than to travel there. What would be the use? My fear is not the height but the sense of insecurity and falling. I don't know if I'll ever be able to overcome this phobia. I've tried many times.

See what I meant about the irony of God taking me right to the edge? And you know what? I never realized the significance of this irony until I started working on this chapter.

Whether it is climbing the fire tower steps, looking out a glass-front elevator, or peering over the library's balcony wall, I always feared the edge and danger. It was *my perception* of the insecurity of the situation that contributed to my fear.

I realize that I did not experience any fear as we walked near the edge of what happened with Eddie. My confidence was first and foremost in God and I knew He was in total control of the circumstances. My faith kept me believing Eddie would be cured here. God has shown me that I was under His wing of protection: "Keep me as the apple of the eye, hide me under the shadow of thy wings" (Psalm 17:8). Verse 5 of that same chapter says, "Hold up my goings in thy paths, *that* my footsteps slip not."

The edge is a scary place. But, if I'm hidden beneath God's protective wing, I can't see what is threatening my safety. Also, if I have used a proper balance of prayer and Bible study, it's easier to have enough wood (faith) to keep the fire going in my heart. In turn, if there is an abundant amount of faith within me, I am secure in knowing that God will keep me from harm (going over the edge).

My heart's desire is to help you (along with me) to understand that even though we must walk near the edge sometimes, there is a safety harness firmly attached to us. There is an unseen wall that will prevent taking the first step into nothingness. Eddie's cancer was threatening my "comfortable" world. God, in His infinite wisdom, did what He knew He had to do to keep my mind safe from going over the edge. It may be a bit unusual, but my God is an unusual God.

# Chapter 10
# WHERE'S THE HOPE?

Discovering hope during times of crisis has to be one of the most difficult things for people to do. The destroyer wants you to feel as though all hope is lost. That's his job ("The thief cometh not, but for to steal, and to kill, and to destroy...." [John 10:10a]). God's job is to lift you up out of the ashes or above those stormy waves. He desires to give life more plentifully ("I am come that they might have life, and that they might have *it* more abundantly" [John 10:10b]). God even assures me in Ephesians 3:20: "Now unto him that is able to do exceeding abundantly above all that we ask or think, according to the power that worketh in us...." It stands to reason that God is capable of what we would think of as "going above and beyond the call of duty." And the fantastic part of this is that He does!

At times I've thought I was hurting too badly to consider discovering hope. All I want to do is think about my pain and how my life has changed. Upon hearing about this book, several of my friends remarked, "Oh, this really must be great therapy for you!"

You know what? It doesn't feel too great right now. It might have felt different if God had told me to write this book a couple of years or so after Eddie's death. There would have been more time to travel through the grief process. Each time I sit down to write, I feel so drained and sad afterward.

It's painful to relive the events leading up to my husband's death. As I scroll up and down the page, I walk those same steps while pouring out my heart to you. As I edit and reedit the same paragraphs, I recall what it took to live those words. Yes, the book may ultimately help my healing process and be a blessing to you *and* me; but during its creation, the pain is recurring. At times it has even been a temporary sacrifice of my peace of mind, but I know it will be worth it in the end.

Deep within my heart is a stirring that I must trust God because He "hath put all things under His feet...." (1 Corinthians 15:27). Think of it as *controlled chaos*. Here's another one of those unbelievable non-contradictions. Even as the winds and the waves rolled and tossed the ship with the disciples (Mark 4:35–41), Jesus had everything under control. Even now, in the middle of this chaos in my life, Jesus has everything under control.

Is it worth the effort and strength to come out of the darkened room, to get up off of the couch, walk out the front door, or rise from my bed to take those steps toward hope? It's been remarkable how God has allowed little, seemingly insignificant events to begin to blow at the pile of these ashes.

Late into the night after Eddie died, our son, Jeremy, and I were at the kitchen table going through pictures to display during the visitation on Sunday night. The walls began to suddenly close in on me. Through my tears and bordering on hysteria, I told Jeremy, "I can't even 'hear' your daddy's voice in my mind any more." That truly upset me! I explained, though, how I had not really heard his dad's "voice" for two years. I had pretty much heard a voice filled with pain, sickness from chemotherapy and radiation, and then in the last couple of days of this life, not at all.

Voices of our friends and family can usually be "heard" in our minds when we replay conversations. Those memories can help us relive events, recall happier times, or bring comfort. I can't put into words the reason for my panic by not being able to recall Eddie's voice in those moments. I can remember feeling ashamed that I could not imagine the sound of his voice, as if he was being erased from my life! Or, it may be that, subconsciously, by hearing his voice I could hold onto him for just a little bit longer. I didn't want to let him go just yet. The intensity level of my pain and grief shot through the roof during those minutes.

I had always prayed that God would give Jeremy His wisdom. I sat dumbfounded listening at the words of comfort pouring from my son's heart.

"Momma, it's OK. There's nothing wrong with you. You'll be able to imagine Daddy's voice again soon. You're exhausted from staying at the hospital. You're just going through a shock right now, your mind is numb, and your pain is stronger than your memory. We've never walked in this valley before, but God's gonna get us through it."

The sound of my son's voice and his words became the healing balm to soothe my hurting heart. I'm the mother. I was supposed to be holding him and telling him it would be all right. But *this* pain couldn't be kissed and made better. Instead, in those minutes, he became the wiser one even in the midst of his own terrible grief.

I sometimes reminisce on different scenes that played out in Eddie's hospital room during his last couple of days. One such time came about on Thursday (June 16) after doctors had delivered the devastating news that Eddie would not leave the hospital. My last recollection of Eddie speaking to us is the loving response he gave to a question. Jeremy happened to be standing by his dad's bedside when he awakened and made a slight groan.

"Daddy, is there anything I can do for you?"

"Take care of your mother for me." Eddie Jones always placed others before himself and he took his commitment to love and care for me very seriously. I was so blessed to have a husband who loved me "as Christ also loved the church…." (Ephesians 5:25) and whose last earthly words were about my care.

Rising early on the following Sunday morning (June 19) and looking ahead toward that night's visitation at the funeral home, the telephone in Eddie's home office rang for some strange reason. Upon placing the receiver to my ear (thinking it might be someone calling the first number in the phone book instead of the second), I heard his company's voice messaging system announcing a new voice mail.

I called the system. The first thing I heard was Eddie's (healthy) voice, stating his name. I entered the password.

The system promptly replied, "There are no new messages in your mailbox."

What (or more importantly, w*ho*) made the telephone ring and incorrectly advise that there were new messages in the mailbox? I know. The Lord knew I needed to hear my husband's voice again to comfort me before that phone number would be permanently disconnected. God had done "exceeding abundantly above all" that I had asked or thought for this special moment. The cool, refreshing breath of God began to blow away some of the ashes on my heart's hearth.

I now sit at his desk working on this book. I glance over from time to time to the silent office telephone that is no longer connected to this world, and I can still hear him from that other world, stating his name just like he did on that beautiful Sunday morning.

There have been other similar experiences since Eddie passed away. These make me rejoice and recall that he did truly exist and was a precious part of my life. You know what else? I can still hear his sweet voice in my mind as clear today as ever.

I can hear him as he would always respond to my "I love you, Honey Bunny," with his "I love you, too, Miss Debby!"

# Chapter 11
# FOR YE HAVE NEED OF PATIENCE...

One weakness I see in my own life, though I'm almost positive others exist (picture a grin and wink here), is my desire to rush God. Over the years, He has truly answered some tremendous prayers for me and a few with relatively quick turnaround.

I met, fell in love with, and married Eddie Jones within six months. God answered my prayer for the right mate quickly. Waiting has never been one of my strong characteristics.

But now, I catch myself wanting to rush the mourning and healing process for my husband's death. Mourning is the pits! Sometimes, I feel like I'm caught between floors in an elevator and somebody's got his hand over the "start" button. I can't go up or down. I'm stuck waiting for help to arrive and our adversary has ripped out the emergency phone. I periodically try to create my own timetable or second-guess God for the months and years ahead.

*Eddie has gone home to be with the Lord and I accept it. That part of my life is complete. So, Lord, if that's the way it is, why can't we move on to the next segment of my life now?*

It's not that I want to forget Eddie or act like he never existed; but, I catch myself asking God to do whatever it is that He's going to do quickly. His promises do not help move me through the grief process any more quickly. In fact, I began to realize that my continual dwelling on them may be a hindrance. God lovingly reins me back in and reminds me that He has a purpose for everything He does or does not do. It's my responsibility to exercise my faith and trust Him that He knows best. I remind myself that when I honestly say to God, "Help me, Lord, to wait," there are going to be times that test my ability to do that.

During my evening prayer time, God has repeatedly told me to "wait." When do you think I'll get the message? I know He wants me to move closer to Him and to trust Him completely. When I try to rush God, I am responding in the flesh and tend to mess up His perfect plan. Isaiah wrote in chapter 55:8–9: "For my thoughts *are* not your thoughts, neither *are* your way my ways, saith the LORD. For *as* the heavens are higher than the earth, so are my ways higher than your ways, and my thoughts than your thoughts." God sees the long-range picture. I try, but my earthly eyes do not have the same perfect perspective as His eyes.

It is even harder to wait on God when He has specifically revealed to you the answer to your prayer but not the timetable for accomplishing the desires of your heart. God tells us in His Word to "Delight thyself also in the LORD; and He shall give thee the desires of thine heart. Commit thy way unto the LORD; trust also in him; and he shall bring *it* to pass" (Psalm 37:4–5).

One night, the Lord showed me another glimpse toward my prayer's answer in Hebrews 10:35–37: "Cast not away therefore your confidence, which hath great recompense of reward. For ye have need of patience, that, after ye have done the will of God, ye might receive the promise. For yet a little while…" My confidence is secure as found in 1 John 5:14–15: "And, this is the confidence that we have in him (God), that, if we ask any thing according to his will, he heareth us: And if we know that he hear us, whatsoever we ask, we know that we have the petitions that we desired of him." I know that God's "little while" and mine are definitely not the same (big sigh inserted here). I'm right back to that timetable issue.

Patience is definitely not one of my strong points. I believe that waiting is one of the hardest things we have to do. We live in an instant world. There are instant foods, instant messaging to one another, instant information through the Internet, and the list goes on and on. We don't want to wait for anything anymore. But, God says that waiting is good and profitable.

Look up the word "wait" in a Bible concordance and see the precious rewards that are available for the waiting. If I wait, then He'll give me the desires of my heart. In the meantime, I have moved closer to Him and learned more about Him. My strongest desire should be to seek God's face. David writes in Psalm 27:8: "*When thou* (God) *saidst*, Seek ye my face; my [David] heart said unto thee (God), Thy face, LORD, will I seek." The petitions or other desires of my heart would be a huge bonus.

During the years I taught Sunday school, I repeatedly told my students that I wanted to be so close to God that I can feel His heartbeat. That's an illustration they can understand, crawling up in Mommy or Daddy's lap and snuggling close enough that their ear is next to their parent's heart. Young ones listen more closely than you may think.

One of my Sunday school kids, Erin Gunnels, wrote back to us in a card (during Eddie's illness): "I miss you and love you both very much. And I hope you get well and are very close w/ God so you can hear his heartbeat."

Being held close and secure is something we can all find encouraging. One of the many things I've missed the most since Eddie died is being held close. I have had the emptiest, achy feeling. I am naturally a "hugging" person. We, as human beings, usually cherish and hunger for that act of love and companionship. Eddie now holds me through the arms of Jeremy and Susan, and our grandchildren (Davis, Will, and Emily).

God also holds me close when my precious ones are not nearby.

# Chapter 12

# IF NOT NOW...WHEN?

OK! So I've taken the first steps toward the hearth of my heart and there seems to be momentum building. But, am I moving too quickly? I have been known to do that on more than one occasion. I want to ask my heavenly Father to just go ahead and blow all of those nasty, hurtful ashes away. I want to say, "You know, God, I've cried buckets of tears over my husband's home-going. Don't you think there's been enough to wash the ashes away?" Let me say once again that we must wait on God.

Permit me to share an example of a special moment with God that happened in 2000. The Lord had clearly shown me He was going to take away some lower back pain for me. He just didn't tell me when. There seems to be a pattern emerging here (grin). As I was coming out to get in my car to go to work on April 15 (that's an ominous day of the year for US citizens, isn't it?), I somehow twisted my body and without stopping to think, I blurted out, "God, I thought You promised that You were going to heal my back!"

The morning started out as partly cloudy. I was in a semi-ill mood and began the twelve-mile drive to work. As I neared the place outside of town where the two lanes turn into a four-lane road, I saw a magnificent rainbow in the sky. I gasped as I looked ahead to the two lanes of my side of the road. I couldn't believe what I was seeing! The rainbow was actually coming down and ending in the right lane where I was driving!

My heart felt like it was going to jump out of my chest. The car drove through the rainbow's end. A feeling of peace and assurance instantly flooded my soul. I wanted to back up, pull off onto the shoulder, and just sit in the rainbow. I knew I had been in the presence of God. I also immediately thought about the rainbow's story in Genesis 9:13–15. Each time we see a rainbow, we are to remember God's covenant (His promise). God knew I didn't just need to see the rainbow but feel it. We see rainbows all the time. However, I did something that day that I've never heard of before. I found the rainbow's end, and yes, there was gold there. It was the precious golden nuggets of God's peace, His promise, His assurance, and His love. There are no other treasures more priceless than these. In addition, a few weeks later,

He fulfilled the promise of what He said He would do and my back was pain-free.

A scary example of "If not now, when?" came about on July 19, 2006, when I went to the doctor's office with nausea and fever. My treatment included a shot of an antibiotic that I had previously received in March for a sinus infection. In my mind I recall leaving the office and getting in my vehicle. I clearly remember backing out of my parking space and stopping at the bottom of the hill to wait for oncoming traffic to pass. I also noted that no cars were present in front of my friends' store, Joy Christian Supplies. *Oh, it's still too early for them to be open since I was at the clinic when they opened at 8:00 A.M.*

The most important point that continued in my mind was that I kept repeating, *Wow, that shot was great! I feel so much better.* As I neared and passed by my building at Jax State, I can recall saying over and over again, "I'm on my way home. I'm feeling good. I'm on my way home." But, I can never recall reaching my house in Piedmont. I can never picture myself getting any closer than the city limits sign.

Dear friend, I was truly on my way home—just not to Piedmont. This time, the reaction to the medication caused instantaneous anaphylactic shock, and I actually never left the clinic in an upright position. The nurse practitioner told me later that it was the worst seizure she had ever seen and that I should not have reacted that soon. Normally, I would have either been in my SUV or back at home when I "seized." My blood pressure dropped to 40/20, my heart stopped, and I am told that CPR was administered. The rescue squad transported me to nearby Jacksonville Hospital where I was stabilized and ultimately transferred to Northeast Alabama Regional Medical Center in Anniston to make sure that I had not suffered a heart attack, since the reaction should not have occurred that quickly.

Yes, my recollection of the events is so real that it took several episodes of explanations to convince me of what actually happened. God was not ready for me to come home. If I had been in my SUV or at home, I would not have survived the allergic reaction. I don't know when my time on this earth will be finished, but I am certain that God left me here for a purpose. To complete this book, perhaps? To fulfill a couple of promises that He has made during my prayer time? Whatever His plan, He could have just as easily carried me on to Heaven on July 19, but He chose not to do so. I am once again humbled by this knowledge that He is not finished with me. There is a purpose to my remaining present in this body.

A rose quickly discovered among those scary ashes is the assurance of the phrase I kept uttering, "I'm on my way home." I knew where I was headed and was looking forward to getting there. "Yea, though I walk through the valley of the shadow of death, I will fear no evil: for thou *art* with me; thy rod and thy staff they comfort me" (Psalm 23:4). I felt no fear, just the somewhat euphoric anticipation of getting home.

"Therefore *we are* always confident, knowing that, whilst we are at home in the body, we are absent from the LORD" (2 Corinthians 5:6). While I dwell in this fleshly body, I am absent from the Lord's presence. However, He is not absent from me. "For ye are the temple of the living God; as God hath said, I will dwell in them, and walk in *them*...." (2 Corinthians 6:16). He is with me because He is in me. I made sure of that on August 23, 1964, when I asked Jesus Christ to be my Savior.

Yes, I am absent from His presence for a season. That will change one day. I will stand in His presence and God, Himself, will welcome me home.

I may be too eager to find this rose before it is ready to be found. It may be that God wants me to have the larger, fully-opened flower and not the small rosebud. If I try to take the rose too soon, then I will miss out on the perfect plan God had intended for me. He could also have more than one rose under the pile of ashes like he did before. Throughout this valley, God has continued to reassure me that He is the one in control and He'll let me know when to take the next step.

Can I possibly tell you how to determine the perfect time for you go to the hearth of your heart to search for the rose? No. That must be between God and you. My time is between God and me. It may take baby steps. It may take several steps. It may take one giant step. I may have to ask (like the children's game), "Father, may I?" I believe God will impart a peace about moving forward, taking that step. I've learned that taking those steps is a part of the ashes disappearing from the hearth of my heart.

# Chapter 13

# REMNANT ASHES, TOO!

Remnants. Bits and pieces. Odds and ends. Leftovers. We can all identify with these words or phrases. It is amazing how I have been blessed to live so many years without having great piles of remnant ashes on the hearth of my heart. You may not have been that fortunate.

While it's true that I've had ashes in the past, I believe they were eventually blown or washed away.

My first engagement was called off because of a great tragedy and there were remnant ashes for many years. I experienced nightmares around the yearly date of the crime and couldn't bring myself to talk about what happened. But now, those years feel like they belonged to someone else. It gets easier to share about that episode in my life. Those ashes are gone forever. I am of the opinion that not all ashes (trials) leave lasting or permanent remnants. I guess that it must depend on the circumstances and what God needs me to learn.

Sometimes a scattering of ashes must remain part of my life. God is using this to complete His plan for me.

Jeremy and I have lived through all of the "firsts" without his dad: first Thanksgiving, first Christmas, first birthdays, the birth of Jeremy and Susan's twins (Will and Emily), and other special occasions.

Davis, our eldest grandson, turned one year old on Eddie's birthday of August 20. Davis's first birthday was certainly bittersweet, but we were determined not to let Eddie's absence overshadow this special day. Christmas of 2005 saw us changing our family's Christmas Eve get-together to Jeremy and Susan's home, and I spent the night with them to celebrate Christmas Day with Susan's family. This was so different from years past, but new traditions had to be made. Father's Day 2006 marked the first anniversary of Eddie's home-going, and looking at the roses I placed on our center altar at church that day did not hurt as much as I thought it would.

Eddie wasn't at church a few weeks later when Jeremy, Susan, and the children surprised me after Sunday school at my church so that Jeremy's "childhood church family" could see Davis, Emily, and Will. By the grace of God, *we made it*! And I am reassured knowing that each celebration will get just a little bit easier to handle. It doesn't mean that we won't ever stop missing Eddie or wishing he was with us. There will always be that hurt described as the speck in the eye that can't be seen but you know it's there just the same. The intense sorrow and pain felt during that first year will begin to lessen as the cycle of life continues.

Can I live with remnant ashes? That's a big, resounding yes! I do it every day. What I choose to do with the remnant ashes is up to me. God comes to me as the Holy Comforter to bring peace the world cannot understand. Remnant ashes can contribute to my testimony. I believe that permanent remnant ashes most commonly represent a loved one's death. It's hard for me to think of anything else that might happen in life that would surpass that kind of grief.

Long-term remnant ashes could possibly be the events of a personal tragedy such as actions surrounding my broken first engagement. The bulk of those ashes were gradually washed away with the cleansing tears. God then lovingly blew the remainder away over the years.

You and God are the only people who know all about your ashes. Think about the times ashes have piled upon the hearth of your heart and their status. Can you make a conscious effort to deal with long-term or permanent remnant ashes?

## MY ASHES CHECKLIST

It may be helpful to you to identify "ashes" in your life. You may even be surprised that there are ashes. This checklist can help you realize that there truly are "ashes" on the "hearth of your heart." Some of the questions may seem redundant, but if the same answer keeps popping up, we know we have ashes.

1. Has there been a recent traumatic event (e.g., death, illness, broken relationship) that interrupted or changed the "normal" course of my life?
   - Does the aftermath of that event leave me with a feeling of despair?
2. Did I think something was going to turn out one way, only to find it went another?
3. Do I feel like I'm drowning, getting too tired to tread water and no one on the shore will throw me a life preserver?
   - Does it feel like I'm all alone in this world?
4. Are there problems (i.e., financial, work-related, etc.) in my life that appear to be impossible to overcome?
   - What kind of feelings occupy my heart *right now*?
5. Can I determine if these feelings are temporary, or have they set up permanent residency?

- What caused these feelings?
- Was the cause my responsibility or outside of my control?
6. Is it possible that I have "remnant" ashes? Can I accept their long-term residency or possible permanency?

# Roses

# Chapter 14

# HE GAVE ME ROSES!

Oh, the beauty of a flawless rose! I've seen buds that required a touch to assure that they were actually real. Then, there have been blossoms I was afraid to hold in my hand because I was fearful I might mar their perfection. In our society, roses represent beauty, grace, and exquisiteness. A bouquet of long-stem roses is generally given to commemorate special occasions, and their price is usually greater than other flowers in God's creation.

God even refers to His Son, Jesus Christ, as the "Rose of Sharon" as found in the Song of Solomon 2:1. Another Old Testament reference to a rose is in Isaiah 35:1–2: "The wilderness and the solitary place shall be glad for them; and the desert shall rejoice, and blossom as the rose. It shall blossom abundantly, and rejoice even with joy and singing; the glory of Lebanon shall be given unto it, the excellency of Carmel and Sharon, they shall see the glory of the Lord, *and* the excellency of our God."

A bouquet of roses is typically given for a special occasion and they are usually expensive. Imagine that. Have you ever noticed that roses cost more around February 14 than at other times of the year? My husband always sent me roses for our wedding anniversary, February 12, instead of Valentine's Day. "It's the principle of the thing!" he said.

My funny, loving husband would gladly pay the higher dollars for roses to celebrate our wedding anniversary but not for Valentine's Day two days later. You might say it's six of one, half a dozen of the other. You're right. It's pay now or pay later. Well, that's just the way Eddie thought and the choice he made about buying a bouquet of roses for me. For many years, he asked the florist to send me different varieties of roses, not the common red ones. He wanted something extra special for me. I've had colors of roses I didn't even know existed. Then other years, he would send the lovely red roses.

The Lord has done the same for me. I've had some of the usual blessings and then several extraordinary ones.

I can't, however, choose how or when I'll pay the price of a rose among the ashes. Only God knows. You see, I honestly believed that Eddie's healing would occur in this life and that we would share many more wedding anniversaries. I told anyone who would listen. Did God lie to me or mislead me? *No!* I've earnestly prayed and agonized over this question and how to describe it here. His answer has poured through my fingers as I type.

If God had revealed to me in 2003 that Eddie would not be cured on Earth, I know from the absolute depths of my heart that I would not have taken another step. I might have even been tempted to turn from God instead of reaching for Him. In His infinite wisdom, God knew that it would take me two years to be able to look Eddie in the face at his bedside, let him go, and tell him "goodbye." He knew that it would take me two years to be able to accept His will and to walk forward (Jeremiah 16:21).

Don't get me wrong. I'm neither perfect nor a super Christian. I cry and have moments where it feels like my heart is going to burst into a million pieces. But, it's during those feelings that I cry out to my heavenly Father. When I cry out to Him, He responds immediately with just what I need. My heart's desire is to seek the face of God, first; and second, for those around me to see Jesus working in me. My desire is to be used of God to minister to others.

The next thing God showed me was this. I proclaimed loud and often that God would cure Eddie in this life. Just ask anyone who knows me. Now, those who heard those words are watching to see how I am handling the different outcome. I was hesitant to delve too deeply into this issue because I was afraid I wouldn't be able to help you understand what happened. I don't know if I can ever fully explain it. All I can confidently say is that I don't want you to be afraid to trust God or believe His promises. Don't think that every time God tells you one way, it will go another. I deeply believe that God looked down in time and saw how I would respond to His "this once."

I am being perfectly honest with myself and you. I believed with every fiber of my being that Eddie and I would live many more years together. Even when he was at his sickest from the cancer treatments, I didn't worry. I re-read Jeremiah 16:21: "Therefore, behold, I will this once cause them to know, I will cause them to know my hand and mine might; and they shall know that my name *is* The LORD."

The miracle came not in Eddie's health, but in how I handled the disappointment. I had to deal with my personal lack of understanding and the tremendous emotional pain accompanying all of it. I recall crying and asking God to help me understand my perception of this total reversal of the outcome. I wanted to keep Eddie with us. But God changed my heart and made it OK, not that my husband died but that God wants to use this for His honor and glory. If I had had my way, God would have given Jeremy and me a detailed accounting as to why Eddie wasn't cured of his cancer. I felt like ordering a complete diagram of God's big picture. Yes, my sinful flesh told me that this would provide the understanding I needed and ease my suffering. In the early days following Eddie's death, I must admit I tried to persuade God to give me a full accounting of just what was going on. Yes, that was certainly what *I* knew I needed.

After several of my selfish prayers, it finally dawned on me to search God's Scriptures, which slowly began to show the answers I sought—not the ones I was demanding of God, but what He wanted to instill in me for more spiritual growth.

"Shew me thy ways, O Lord; teach me thy paths. Lead me in thy truth, and teach me: for thou *art* the God of my salvation; on thee do I wait all the day. Remember, O Lord, thy tender mercies and thy loving kindnesses; for they *have been* ever of old. Remember not the sins of my youth, nor my transgressions: according to thy mercy remember thou me for thy goodness' sake, O Lord" (Psalm 25:4–7).

The psalmist David spoke these words and God used them to reassure me that His ways are the best ones, His paths are the only sure paths, His truth is the only one that will stand. He taught me this during those hours with Him. Like David, He is the God of my salvation and I will wait on Him to show me what he wants me to know. It is because of His everlasting tender mercies and lovingkindness that He will show me. David entreated the Lord not to hold the sin against him, and I asked God to forgive me for my demands. I asked Him to have mercy on me, not for the sake of my goodness but His alone.

I am now at peace in trusting that God carried my precious husband to Him because his journey on this earth was finished. Every day has worked together to bring me to the acceptance of the different outcome and letting go. I believe that Eddie knew before Jeremy and I did when he sought Jeremy's promise with, "Take care of your mother for me." I believe it's called "dying grace." There may be more to the big picture that I can't see just now, but what God has shown me satisfies the longing to understand and that God will always be there to take care of us.

Some treasured roses I have found among the ashes include: a gospel music ministry when I was a single young woman, which led me to a wonderful and perfect-for-me husband from February 12, 1977, to June 18, 2005; a talented and loving son; a precious daughter-in-law and three grandchildren; an anticipated ministry of encouragement to cancer patients and their spouses; a life filled to the brim with joy, love, laughter, family, and friends; and, more recently, this book of inspiration and hope to you. I am eternally grateful to my heavenly Father for these roses.

# Chapter 15

# DO INSTRUCTIONS COME WITH IT?

How do you find a rose among ashes? How *do* you discover hope when there doesn't seem to be any? How can I put something intangible into words for you to understand what I know deep inside of me? How can I possibly introduce to you that which I sometimes take for granted?

In a conversation with my precious pastor, Brother Danny English, I shared my dilemma with him. I stated that this was the hardest part of the book I've had to write. I have truly struggled with knowing everything God wants me to share with you. Just because the Lord tells you to write a book, it doesn't mean that all of the thoughts and answers will come easily. God is also bringing me through a process.

A piece of paper with the scribbled phrase, "how to find the hope," lies beside the keyboard as I write. I look at the paper and then over to a framed photo of Eddie and me taken in La Jolla, California, with a spectacular view of the ocean and sky behind us. The sun is setting, clouds are gathering across the twilight sky, and we are smiling at our dear friends (Mike and Susan Mayo) who capture this moment in time. At first glance, in this picture, Eddie will always be healthy and young. As I sit here and write, from time to time I have looked at that picture more deeply and with a different eye. There are some darker clouds becoming more visible in the background as we are holding each other and smiling into the camera. Little did we know that dark clouds were gathering in our lives. As I reflect back, I slowly realize that Eddie's cancer was surely already growing in his body. Even though the storm clouds were about to blow us to and fro, Jesus had it under control.

Hope is one of those words that brings a smile to my face as I say it (kind of like the word "chocolate" for most of us girls!). I don't consider hope as a "maybe" sort of word. You might say it's almost looking at the glass as half full or half empty. I view the word "hope" as the assurance of a particular matter.

The apostle Paul wrote in 1 Corinthians 15:19: "If in this life only we have hope in Christ, we are of all men most miserable." Friend, I have the assurance of Christ in this life *and* the one to come. So how can I be miserable? I'm not. That doesn't mean I don't feel sadness and loneliness. As we say in the South, "I just ain't gonna waller around in it." Sadness is temporary. Misery or bitterness is long-term. I can't find the hope if I'm miserable and bitter. God says, "Happy *is he* that *hath* the God of Jacob for his help, whose hope *is* in the LORD his God" (Psalm 146:5).

So, how *do* you find hope in the face of adversity? Trust is a key component in finding that hope. "For thou *art* my hope, O LORD God: *thou art* my trust from my youth" (Psalm 71:5). That verse has both words in it! Talk about a double promise! David proclaimed that God was his hope *and* trust. In order to experience the hope, I trust God's promises. I believe them with all of my heart. "For all the promises of God in him *are* yea, and in him Amen, unto the glory of God by us" (2 Corinthians 1:20). The prophet Jeremiah wrote, "Blessed *is* the man that trusteth in the LORD, and whose hope the LORD is" (Jeremiah 17:7). If I trust in the Lord and my hope is in Him, then God says I am blessed.

> Lord, give me faith—to live from day to day.
> Lord, give me faith— to trust, if not to know.
> Lord, give me faith—to leave it all to thee.[3]

As I had already shared with you, the wood on the hearth of my heart represents my faith. Wood on the hearth, like faith, can be stacked up and ready to use.

But, think about this. If it just lies there, what good is it? Faith has always been an important part of my life, even before I made the choice to surrender my life to Jesus Christ.

My precious, prayer warrior mother, Willie Mae Fields, related a story to me several years ago that I did not even remember. The following is taken from her handwritten account.

> When I have a very urgent prayer request or need a special touch from God, I often go into my bedroom, close the door and kneel down beside my bed. Many years ago, when my daughter Debby was only five and a half years old, I prayed for her to be healed and received a miracle for her.
>
> Debby had received a bad sunburn on her back while we were on a vacation in Florida. After we came home she broke out in blisters on her back and as they dried out, she began to itch. I put ointments, creams, and home remedies on her skin but she still itched a lot. Finally, I gave up and told her I would just have to take her to the doctor. She calmly replied, "You can pray and ask God to heal me." I hesitated for a few seconds not knowing exactly what to say. I didn't want her to be disappointed in her child-like faith if she wasn't healed immediately.
>
> But I said, "I sure will pray for you, Baby."

## Do Instructions Come With It?

Later, when I had time to be alone, I went into my bedroom and knelt down beside my bed. I began praying, "Dear God, you know Debby is just a little child but she believes you will heal her and I'm asking you to give a special miracle of healing. She won't understand if she is not healed."

That was a far as I got in my prayer. A golden glow filled the room and the hairs on my arms and head stood on end. My eyes were still closed as I saw a white robed figure walk slowly past me. I reached my hand out toward the robe to touch it (Matthew 9:20–22), and I knew that God would answer my prayer and heal my little girl.

I remembered in the Bible that not everyone was healed instantly, but even if it was not His will to give her this miracle right away, I would not question it. My vision faded after a few seconds but I was never the same after that Holy experience.

The next morning as I helped her out of her pajamas and into her clothes, I told myself I would not look or touch her back but I accidentally touched her and was amazed that her skin was as smooth as it was before the blisters! I told Debby, "God answered my prayer! Your back is healed."

And, she said, "I knew He would if you prayed for me." We hugged each other again, enjoying the special miracle from God, a special one-of-a-kind blessing.

Faith seemed to evolve naturally for me. I was blessed to be brought up in a Christian home. My paternal grandfather was a Baptist preacher, and I can recall traveling with him and my grandmother as he preached revivals during the summertime. Not everyone is as fortunate as I to have such a rich Christian heritage. For others, faith frequently grows the hard way...on-the-job training!

That same evening, Brother Danny (my pastor), Mrs. Remona (his wife), and I also talked about faith in our conversation around their kitchen table. After I left them, God spoke to my heart to give me a simple meaning of faith. He said, "Faith is when the heart says yes even though the brain says no."

My friend, faith is the heart believing that there *is* a rose buried beneath those ashes, even though your head tells you that a rose could not survive under them. Don't you see that only a "rose" of God's could be found among a pile of ashes?

I glanced back over several verses that God had given me one year prior to Eddie's home-going. I know now what those verses mean more clearly than when He showed me. "I will visit you, and perform my good word toward you, in causing you to return to this place. For I know the thoughts that I think toward you, saith the LORD, thoughts of peace, and not of evil, to give you an expected end. Then shall ye call upon me, and ye shall go and pray unto me, and I will hearken unto you. And ye shall seek me, and find *me*, when ye shall search for me with all your heart" (Jeremiah 29:10–13). As mentioned earlier about ashes, this scripture reinforces that I should seek God with my whole heart as my top priority.

Let me remind you of Psalm 57:7: "My heart is fixed, O God, my heart is fixed: I will sing and give praise." I know how hard it is to sing and give praise when your heart is burdened. Focus on all of the good things in your life. Praise may come easier than you suppose. Praise is another avenue to finding hope in troubles. When I praise the living God even for just who He is, my praise acts as a cool, refreshing breeze and begins to scatter the ashes.

That's how you discover hope in the aftermath of trials. I tried so very hard to come up with several ways to share with you. I didn't want to miss anything. I kept telling myself that I must present "different strokes for different folks." Not everyone is alike. We're all individuals. But, there is only one way, and it's through God the Father with the Holy Spirit making intercession and taking our groanings to Glory's throne room. He will be to you what you need Him to be. God tells us in Jeremiah 31:3: "Yea, I have loved thee with an everlasting love...." Hebrews 13:8 says, "Jesus Christ the same yesterday, and to-day, and for ever." God proclaimed in Malachi 3:6: "For I *am* the LORD, I change not...."

God knows how to comfort me. Matthew 6:8 states: "for your Father knoweth what things ye have need of, before ye ask him." Well, if God knows what I need, then why do I have to ask? Asking demonstrates my dependency upon Him. Asking helps me align my will with His. I don't pray to change God's will but to change mine.

As it turned out, I did not date during my high school years and only began dating one of my classmates two weeks before our senior prom. I can recall often sitting at home on Friday or Saturday nights, wishing for a Prince Charming who would ride up my driveway and take me away to his castle. It always seemed that my best friends had better luck with young love than I.

During the days following my broken first engagement, an emotional war was raging inside of me. Here I was twenty-one years of age and already had my happily-ever-after plans destroyed. *My chance at love and marriage is gone! What can I do? Will I ever meet anyone else?*

One Saturday afternoon a few months later I was in my bedroom meditating on the Lord after returning home from our quartet's radio broadcast. *God, I've tried so hard to find someone to love and who will love me. But now, I'm gonna wait for you to send me whoever you want me to have. I'll even be content not to date until you send the man you have for me. All I ask is that you let me know somehow when I meet him so that I'll know that it's You doing it and not me.* In essence, I was making sure that my will matched God's; that what I wanted for my life was exactly what God wanted. I was tired of trying to meet someone on my own. I surrendered my will to His that afternoon, which is what I should have been doing all along.

Approximately two weeks following my change of heart, I met Eddie Jones. The rest is history. God had prepared my future; my will just got in the way. But, God used my earlier trial to help me grow stronger in Him. You know what's strange? The Choralaires and The Bridgemen were scheduled to sing at a New Year's Eve service a few months prior to when Eddie and I met. I came down with the flu that afternoon and had to miss the service. God had to wait for me to understand and acknowledge that my will must be His will, that my timetable is His timetable.

# Chapter 16

# YOU WANT ME TO TRUST YOU WITH WHAT, GOD?

Trust God with every aspect of your life. God wants to hear from you in the "little stuff" as well as the "big deal." What matters to you, matters to your heavenly Father. I've even prayed over finding lost files in my office. (It worked, too!)

I think back over the times when I have heard someone pray aloud, "Lord, I pray that you would lead, guide, and direct us." One might think, "Don't they really mean the same thing?" I used to think so. Then, I heard an explanation (from a long-ago former pastor) of the differences in leading, guiding, and directing that made perfect sense to me.

## God Leads Me

That means that He is in front, a concept of me being on His spiritual leash. He's walking ahead of me and also has a hold on me. He is holding on to me and I don't have to fear. I might get tired and let go; He won't.

## The Lord Guides Me

He walks beside me each day. I've observed guide dogs for the visually impaired at the university where I work as they walk beside their person, helping that one who depends on them to know when or where to walk and when to stop. By walking beside me, God can show me things He wants me to see and hear. He may say, "Look over here or over there. Don't miss this!" He can also gently take my arm to stop me if He sees me beginning to walk in the wrong direction or too close to the edge. Also, if the visually-impaired student releases the guide dog's harness, he/she is then on their own to face the walk. Once again, God has a firm hold on me.

## My Heavenly Father Directs Me

That is, He is behind me pointing the way ahead. He has both hands firmly on my shoulders and can give a little nudge in the direction that I need to go. Trusting God with all aspects of my life can be hard to remember. A very wise man, Solomon, wrote in Proverbs 3:6: "In all thy ways acknowledge Him, and He shall direct thy paths." Seems too simple, doesn't it?

My first encounter with trust and hope came on August 23, 1964, when I acknowledged that I needed a Savior, Christ Jesus, the Holy Son of God. I trusted God with my heart and my eternity. I learned how to discover that hope while attending Sunday school, worship service, GA's, Vacation Bible School, and talking to my wonderful mother and grandfather (the Baptist preacher).

"To appoint unto them that mourn in Zion, to give unto them beauty for ashes, the oil of joy for mourning, the garment of praise for the spirit of heaviness; that they might be called trees of righteousness, the planting of the LORD, that he might be glorified" (Isaiah 61:3).

To give you an answer about how to go about finding hope when there doesn't seem to be any, God hasn't given me anything different to give to you outside of Him. *He* is the silver lining in the cloud. *He's* the bright spot on the dark day. Turn to *Him*.

# Chapter 17

# TRADING ASHES FOR ROSES

A rose found among the ashes must not be taken lightly. Don't leave it there (especially if it's a ministry rose). It must be picked. Remember, a rose has a short lifespan. Have you ever had a vase filled with roses that lasted more than just a few days?

Leave the remnant ashes we talked about earlier on the hearth but take the rose. Remember, God's breath will blow and scatter the dry ashes if cleansing tears have not already washed over the hearth of your heart. As I study God's Word and pray, aligning my will with His, He prompts a heavenly breeze to sweep over the hearth of my heart. The ashes of my disappointment or broken dreams begin to spread out.

I cried many, many tears when my first marriage plans were canceled and again years later when Eddie passed away. These haven't been the only tears I've shed; they're just the most heartbreaking in my life that could have affected my relationship with God. So, what kind of tears were they? It is my feeling that immediate reaction tears are simply tears of pain coming from a broken heart.

As the circle of life continues and I begin to establish a new norm without Eddie, some daily experiences tend to bring tears to the surface. What do I do with them? Do I go ahead and cry or refuse to allow them to flow? Tears can be a great release valve for the heart and soul. Women tend to cry, most men don't. Society long ago told men that crying demonstrates a form of weakness for them. Men in the Bible days cried. David cried over the state of his soul. Jeremiah cried over a nation. Jesus wept. God even collects our tears in a bottle (Psalm 56:8).

As time marched on into weeks and months after Eddie died, my immediate grieving tears became cleansing tears. What's the difference? Cleansing tears originate from a broken heart that is desperate and searching to heal. These tears act as a cleansing agent and help move the ashes aside so that God's love can find a lodging place to help the healing process. Cleansing tears help to open up the lines of communication between this heart and the Lord.

Bitter tears stem from a heart that refuses to heal and wants to hold pain in its grasp. That person may tend to lash out at God like Job's wife wanted him to do (Job 2:9). Anger seems to be an emotion that's easier to deal with than sadness. Anger seeks to find a place to lay blame. *God took Eddie instead of healing him on earth. Eddie left me behind.* Anger is like a cancer that eats away at the heart's tenderness and receptiveness.

I've studied the bare, hard ground in front of the gazebo in my yard. This is where Jeremy's dog once lived on a chain until close friends Casey and Lori Ponder gave him a home in the countryside where he can now run and play freely. Grass is struggling to grow back, but the soil is packed down like concrete. I know that it will be better to break up the ground so that the existing grass will spread or new grass seed can be sown.

Jesus tells the parable of the sower in Matthew 13:3–9. Seeds were sown in different areas: by the wayside, on stony places, among thorns, and in good ground. Just like the story that Jesus shares and my own area in front of the gazebo, the ground must be prepared to receive the seeds for anything healthy to sprout.

Bitter tears gush from the wayside, stony places, and among thorns—a heart that has determined to be rebellious and shut God out. Cleansing tears flow from the good ground—a heart that runs to God, not from Him. Once again, I must choose how I respond to the ashes. Do I harden my heart so that bitter tears only pack down the ashes? Or, have I spent quality fellowship time with God so that my heart automatically searches for what God has planned for me when I emerge from this valley of hurt?

Permanent remnant ashes will linger. There will always be pain associated with the death of my husband. Some of those ashes will continue to remain on the hearth of my heart as long as I am in this body. But over time, the pile of ashes (if I choose) will grow smaller as the rose emerges.

Recall the two imaginary rooms described in chapter one. The first room is inviting and draws you in. It's not hard to walk over to the comforting fireplace to bask in the warmth it provides. In fact, you usually run to it. That fireplace could represent a heart that is filled with God and loving Him. Or, it could represent a life that is experiencing everything going your way. Sooner or later, if the wood on the hearth (representing faith) is not replenished, it's going to run out and the fire will die from lack of fuel. Also, the hearth might be filled with wood; yet, if I don't use equal amounts of wood and tools (faith, prayer, and Bible study), then that wood will eventually be used up or the fire will slowly burn itself out from a lack of being tended. I can picture in my mind how Eddie worked the coals prior to adding more wood so that it enabled the fire to continue burning brightly.

Without proper attention, you may find yourself in the second room described in chapter one. Think again about the questions the woman asks aloud. Do they sound familiar? I know they did to me. I believe that I've asked them on more than one occasion.

I learned the hard way about not replenishing the wood and using the tools properly to keep the flames strong and roaring. I told you in chapter five about not being able to pray for Eddie until I had prayed for myself. God then broke the chains that were binding me. I had neglected prayer time and Bible study, as well as "alone" time with God. Though I may have tons of faith, I must also tend the fire with my spiritual tools so that I ensure that my will is aligned with God's. I don't ever want to travel back down that lonely road again!

Friend, God did not promise the Christian's life would be without heartache. He did promise He would be with us each step of the way.

A rose is given for special occasions. How *special* to know that for each trial there is a blessing and sometimes more than one. That traumatic event or problem in your life has produced a rose. Only you will discover what the rose will be this time. God will tell you.

## My Roses Checklist

Earlier, I talked about praising God for His blessings. How can this help when I'm trying to discover hope in the middle of tragedy? Take a few moments to think about some roses you may have found in your pile of ashes. Record your very special personal roses.

- Have I experienced a new or more personal relationship with Jesus Christ?
- Have I gained a wonderful and close friendship?
- Did God bring someone into my life whom I might not have met otherwise?
- Did my crisis result in a ministry that I had never dreamed of?
- Was a husband/wife a blessing from a trial?
- Was the "rose" a desired, precious child?
- Did I realize a closer walk with the Lord?
- Was a new job provided?
- Did God answer a prayer?
- Can you think of some others that are not included here?

# A Special Message from Debby

"Who comforteth us in all our tribulation, that we may be able to comfort them which are in any trouble, by the comfort wherewith we ourselves are comforted of God" (2 Corinthians 1:4).

When my heavenly Father spoke to my heart about writing this book to you, my husband had been undergoing cancer treatment since early 2003. Writings began around March 18, 2005, and I did not even begin to imagine what his "healing" would be.

My faith stayed firmly upon his earthly cure until the doctors told us the afternoon of June 16 that he would not leave the hospital. We could not keep count of the friends who came to his room during that Thursday night and Friday, reeling with the shock that Eddie would not survive this third occurrence of cancer. As his earthly family surrounded his bedside in the waning minutes of June 17, Jeremy and I each held one of his cherished hands and continuously assured him that we loved him. We told him we would be OK as he left this world for the one "whose builder and maker is God." We would see him again. Eddie's "healing" came at 12:05 A.M. on June 18.

Just a few weeks before, God had spoken words to my heart taken from the story of Lazarus in John 11:4: "This sickness is not unto death." A close friend and brother in Christ, Jerry Sanford, had been so wonderful to help us at home. Many times he took Eddie for chemo and radiation so I could keep working during those two years. I had shared these words with Jerry and his wife Rhonda, as well as our church, family, and friends. Over the next couple of days afterward, Jerry shared with me how he cried out to God that Sunday (June 19) trying to understand what had happened. Wanting to comfort me and help me to also understand, Jerry said that God spoke to his heart and reassured him with these exact words: "This sickness is *not* unto death, but unto life."

Ashes have once again returned to the hearth of my heart. I must decide in my heart as to whether I will let the Father's holy breath scatter them or permit bitter tears to harden them into a "crust." It's a choice God has given me the freedom to make. I took that first step and God has taken the others with me. But, I can honestly assure you that it never entered my mind not

## A Special Message from Debby

to take the first step. You see, He's never failed me and never will.

If you doubt you have the strength or even the desire to make that first step, I promise you it can be done. You see, it's not a promise made by me but by God—a God who cannot fail. It may be that you don't feel like you have much faith. Or you may feel like you have not lived the kind of life where you believed in what faith can accomplish. Wouldn't you at least like to give God a try and see what He can do?

I'm truly excited about what lies ahead for me. Yes, I miss Eddie and always will. A scattering of remnant ashes will have a permanent place on the hearth of my heart. He was a rose among the ashes with a short lifespan. I don't understand why he had to leave me at age fifty-five. But, I'll tell you a secret. He's sitting right beside Jesus in my heart. He's cheering me on. He's encouraging me to take one step, the next, and the one after that. If the truth be known, his love mingled with my faith to encourage me to take that first step toward looking for the rose among this pile of ashes.

I don't know all that God has planned for me, but I do know that it will be a perfect rose—one without blemish or flaw. Who knows? Once again, there may even be more than one rose hidden among the ashes!

# More and More Roses

When one tells the story of personal tragedy and triumph in his or her life, it doesn't come without earthly help. The friends and family I have already named throughout the pages of *A Rose Among the Ashes* were included because God directed me to share the unique or special part they played. However, there are certain additional people in my life whom I must recognize for their love and support as these ashes piled into a heap. I know that for the vast majority of this book's readers, they will simply be names on a page and nothing more. But, on the hearth of my heart they will *always* be an entire garden of roses.

Time and time again I have tried to thank my spiritual family of Northside Baptist Church in Piedmont, Alabama. They know all of the acts of kindness (too numerous to mention) that they did for us and so does God. Your love and compassion will not go unrewarded in Heaven (Matthew 25:40).

In addition, I am also grateful for the other church congregations in Piedmont and the surrounding areas who offered up prayers on our behalf. Prayer is one of the greatest commitments that can be made for each other. May God richly bless each one who ever uttered a word of prayer for Eddie, Jeremy, and me.

My director, co-workers, and friends at Jacksonville State University enabled me to do what I had to do during 2003-2005. Their kindness, understanding, and support will never be forgotten.

The extraordinary and talented men—Jerry Gilley, Ivan Ray, and Jeff Haney—who made up The Bridgemen Quartet with Eddie as I know them, along with their wives and children, will always be a part of my extended family, no matter where God leads me from here. We traveled many miles together before and during our marriages to do what God had asked, to carry His gospel in song.

Linda Gilden, a talented and published author in her own right. Linda, God used you to provide the guidance and assistance that I would need to do His bidding. While we may never see each other face-to-face in this life, we shall kneel together around our Father's throne in the one to come. May God richly bless your own work and ministry.

Mandi Reynolds eagerly and lovingly provided a fresh set of eyes to proof the manuscript. Our friendship has spanned the years of initially being church family, then as she was a student assistant in my office during her college years at Jax State, and now in a deeper and more treasured friendship.

And then there are two special families who became like our own from the time God brought the two teen-aged young men into our lives. They are Kevin and Carlos Farmer (twins), their wives (Candice and Tiffany, respectively), and their children (Sarah and Noah and Tyler and Emily, respectively). Listing everything they've done for us and continue to do for Jeremy and me would create an entire chapter in this book. Suffice it to say that they are truly a part of the Jones family by choice and were born of blood, the blood of Jesus Christ.

Last, but surely not the least, you, the reader of *A Rose Among the Ashes*. You may have purchased this book for yourself or someone may have selected it for you for a particular reason. I hope that it provided something that you needed. There may come a time when ashes will be piled upon the "hearth of your heart" and you need to find a rose. Most importantly, I pray that God spoke to your heart about "discovering hope when there doesn't seem to be any."

I can never thank all of you enough. I'll just have to let God do it for me. Besides, He can do a much greater job than I. After all, I'm just His typist.

My lips shall ever utter praise and adoration to the One who cares for me and takes such great care of me, my faithful heavenly Father. *Thank you, sweet Lord, for all of my beautiful roses and the ones to come.*

—Debby Fields Jones

# THE BEST ROSE OF ALL!

I would not want you to close the cover of *A Rose Among the Ashes* and place it on a shelf or in a drawer without encouraging you to have the "best rose of all." I am, of course, referring to Jesus Christ, the Son of God.

We've talked about the heart, ashes, and roses among these pages. These also paint a picture of God's salvation. There's head knowledge and then there's heart knowledge. For the first nine years of my life I had heard lesson after lesson and sermon after sermon on the plan of salvation, how Jesus had died for me, and the Christian's life. I knew Bible verses by memory (head knowledge), but until that beautiful August Sunday morning I had not translated it into heart knowledge. In a matter of moments, the Holy Spirit miraculously took the Bible verses I had learned and helped me to acknowledge that

I was the "whosoever" that is mentioned in John 3:16: "For God so loved the world, that He gave His only begotten Son, that whosoever believeth in Him should not perish, but have everlasting life."

If you know that God exists and His Son, Jesus, "gave himself a ransom for all" (1 Timothy 2:6), you may not have yet moved from head knowledge to that of the heart. It could even be that you've never heard the wonderful gospel of Jesus Christ before, and now something has stirred within you to make you want to know more.

I asked Jesus to be my Lord on August 23, 1964. I was nine years old on that day and felt the Holy Spirit tugging at my heart's strings to be saved. I surrendered and walked forward to kneel in the altar of my church to pray. My dad, who is also at home with the Lord and was already at the altar praying, saw me and shouted with joy. That was the most important decision in my life and it has never been regretted.

Without Jesus Christ as my personal Savior, I could not have had the courage to approach any of the ashes in my life to take the roses. I invite you to look deep inside yourself and compare yourself to the three segments of this little book.

## The Heart

The inner core of our being where life's feelings exist. It's where commitments are made, too ("for the

Lord your God proveth you, to know whether ye love the Lord your God with all your heart and with all your soul" [Deuteronomy 13:3]). What comes from the lips, starts in the heart ("for out of the abundance of the heart the mouth speaketh" [Matthew 12:34]).

## The Ashes

Though we are His creation, God's Word specifically tells us that we are dead in our trespasses and sin and nothing is of value outside of Him. Our lives are just remnants scattered about waiting to be pulled together into something beautiful.

"And you, being dead in your sins and the uncircumcision of your flesh, hath he quickened together with him, having forgiven you all trespasses; Blotting out the handwriting of ordinances that was against us, which was contrary to us, and took it out of the way, nailing it to his cross" (Colossians 2:13–14).

Confess that you are a sinner, without hope, and you need Jesus as your Savior.

Once we come to the realization that there is only one way to eternal life in the presence of Almighty God, it is then that we find the beauty among the ashes of our lives.

## The Rose

Jesus Christ, the Holy Son of God, who gave His life willingly to pay the price for our salvation: "And this is the record, that God hath given to us eternal life, and this life is in his Son" (1 John 5:11). Believe who He is (the Son of God), what He did (died on Calvary's cross to pay for our sin), and where He is (rose from the grave and is seated at the right hand of God the Father).

Salvation is simple. God didn't make it hard, though sometimes we do. You don't even have to be in a church to accept Jesus as your Savior. If God is dealing with your heart at this moment, don't delay. The Bible says that "Now *is* the accepted time; now *is* the day of salvation" (2 Corinthians 6:2). God speaks in Romans 10:10: "For with the heart man believeth unto righteousness; and with the mouth confession is made until salvation." Confess to the Lord that you are without hope and your eternal destiny is doomed. Ask Him to forgive you and save you. Living a life in Jesus is absolutely the best "rose" of all until we reach eternity in Heaven!

Maybe you can recall a time when you asked Jesus to be your Savior, but the ashes on the hearth of your heart have become a hardened "crust." Confess the sin that created the crust; ask Him right now to chisel away at that crust, and restore you to full fellowship with Him. "He restoreth my soul...." (Psalm 23:3a). "Restore unto me the joy of thy salvation...." (Psalm 51:12a). God is absolutely in the restoration business!

Jesus Christ is truly the best rose of all, an everlasting "Rose of Sharon" who will never forsake you. I invite you to turn to Him at this very moment.

# Endnotes

1. *Sitting at the Feet of Jesus* (Author Unknown, Public Domain, *Select Hymns*, 1911).
2. *The Prayer Life,* Andrew Murray, Fleming H. Revell, p.88 (Public Domain).
3. Opening line of each stanza of an untitled prayer by John Oxenham, as published in *Church Bulletin Bits Volume #2, Compiled by George W. Knight.*

www.ingramcontent.com/pod-product-compliance
Lightning Source LLC
Chambersburg PA
CBHW030328080526
44584CB00012B/762